House Rules

House Rules

100 WAYS TO FEEL AT HOME

Emma Beryl Kemper

Illustrations by
Georgie Stewart

UNION
SQUARE
& CO.

NEW YORK

UNION SQUARE & CO.

NEW YORK

UNION SQUARE & CO. and the distinctive Union Square & Co. logo are trademarks of Sterling Publishing Co., Inc.

Union Square & Co., LLC, is a subsidiary of Sterling Publishing Co., Inc.

ISBN 978-1-4549-5201-5
ISBN 978-1-4549-5202-2 (e-book)

For information about custom editions, special sales, and premium purchases, please contact specialsales@unionsquareandco.com.

Printed in China

2 4 6 8 10 9 7 5 3 1

unionsquareandco.com

Editors: Amanda Englander and Caitlin Leffel
Designer: Renée Bollier
Illustrator: Georgie Stewart
Project Editor: Ivy McFadden
Production Manager: Terence Campo
Copy Editor: Megha Jain

To Ben, Rosie, and Caleb:
Home simply isn't home without you.

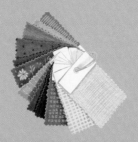

Contents

Introduction

We've all heard the adages "There's no place like home," "Home is where the heart is," and "Home sweet home." Whether or not we prescribe to one of these schools of thought, there's no question that home is an important place to each of us. The meaning of that word, "home," transcends a physical dwelling; it encompasses a feeling of peace and belonging. I believe we can elevate our standards of living by making the most of our homes, designing a space that perfectly suits our needs. Home can even help you achieve your goals. The state of your home reflects the state of your life; a comfortable, functioning home both signals and provides solace.

Successful interior design makes a space most capable of serving its intended purpose. A study can enhance your productivity; a nursery can cocoon a new baby; a kitchen can yield delicious flavors. The way you choose to express your style in these spaces using colors, materials, lighting, and textures, and the way you maximize functionality to meet your needs, is what makes your home uniquely yours.

I have been in love with interior design for as long as I can remember. As a child, I frequently found myself arranging and rearranging the furniture in my bedroom. I'd eagerly offer unsolicited design advice to anyone willing to listen, and I even once "surprised" my parents by painting our bathroom a vibrant lime green. Despite this deep interest, interior design didn't initially occur to me to consider as a feasible career path. After graduating from Tulane University, I opted for a career in the adjacent fashion industry instead. Despite landing a fashion PR role, which I was excited about, the allure of interiors continued to nag at me. After a few years, I found a new position at a company that encompassed both fashion and interior design verticals, and I seized every opportunity to immerse myself in the world of interiors. Eventually, I made the pivotal decision to change the trajectory of my career and headed to the New York School of Interior Design to formally study my—until then—hobby.

I graduated in 2012, worked for a Brooklyn-based boutique design firm, and then in 2015, took a leap of faith and established my eponymous firm, Emma Beryl Interiors. Since then, I've had the privilege of engaging in residential and commercial projects all over the United States. To me, it's a profound honor to be trusted with the responsibility of helping people optimize the most significant spaces in their lives.

It is my design philosophy that a home should be ever-evolving, adapting with you through all the chapters of your life. My goal is for this book to be used as a reference manual and handbook while you're engaged in a particular home improvement project, or it can be read from cover to cover for a more comprehensive understanding of home decor. Either way, *House Rules* will give you all the essential tools you need for building a home that is *your* home. It is a list of my best practices and the design rules I abide by, drawing on my education and experience as an interior designer.

With that said, please bear in mind that while I hope these guidelines offer valuable insight, I also wholeheartedly believe that the magic happens when you feel free to deviate from the rules if and when inspiration strikes. After all, your design choices and expressing what distinctly resonates with you is what will turn your house into your home. My goal is that no matter what phase or season you're in, this book provides the tools to create a home that serves as a rich backdrop to make memories in, and supports you in every design change you implement in your space. It should serve as a trusted hand to hold, reminding you of tried-and-true interior design principles. I hope *House Rules* demystifies the home renovation and design processes and inspires, empowers, and guides you toward discovering your own personal sense of style.

Mood Boards

The first step in designing your home is to find inspiration. I personally enjoy browsing online, perusing interior design and architecture books, scrolling on Instagram, watching movies, and even visiting hotels to find interiors that resonate with me.

They need not all be new discoveries: as you gather images, don't forget to tap into the rich resource that is your own life experience and nostalgia. Consider cherished elements of your childhood home, memories from a special trip, or features of a friend's home that you've always admired. The spaces that have left a significant impact often have a distinct personality and a strong point of view, which will empower you to make

bold choices in your own design. Drawing inspiration from your memories gives your space personality and individuality that would be impossible for anyone else to replicate. Furthermore, examining and honoring your long-term preferences ensures that you stay authentic to your own style, even when you're being inundated with trends on social media.

At this point, don't concern yourself with unraveling the reasons "why" you like something; just save images onto your mood boards for future analysis. This phase is about organically curating a bank of design elements that resonate with you.

Your method of saving these collected images should be one that comes naturally to you and feels easy. For me, Pinterest is a favorite because the images are easy to see together and to keep organized. You could also consider tangible pin-boards, binders, or even saving images in an album on your phone. I dedicate a single mood board to each individual space I am working on. Doing so allows me to examine my project room by room as well as to align the boards to assess the project as a cohesive whole.

Keep Sense of Place Front of Mind

Bear in mind context while collecting your inspiration images. For example, while you might love the aesthetic of a Dutch stone farmhouse, consider that incorporating significant design elements from that style might not work well in your industrial downtown loft. The idea is for your interior design to harmoniously intertwine with the architecture of your home and to fit within the context of your neighborhood. If available, look at older images of your home, watch movies featuring homes similar to yours in location, age, and style, and scour the internet for photos of comparable spaces. If you live in a new-build, identify the architectural style of your house and take a look at similar, older spaces for inspiration. This research is interesting, and it adds a fun intellectual dimension to your renovation when you're able to incorporate subtle references to your home's history into your design. Any nods that you can make to the original architecture of your space will go a long way in making your home feel authentic and will help you avoid trends. (See also Rule #4.) Pay special attention to colors, materials, silhouettes (for faucets, light fixtures, moldings, and tiles), and layouts that were popular around the time your home was built. Attempting to force your home into something it inherently is not will result in a design that feels contrived. The best designs honor the past and embrace history yet feel creative, fresh, and personal.

Play to Your Strengths

It's important to identify and emphasize the distinctive features that initially drew you to your home, whether that is original hardwood flooring, beautiful natural light, or soaring ceiling heights. Consider how your design choices can help accentuate these characteristics and collect images that showcase spaces with comparable qualities to help you tell the story of what you love about your home through strategic selections. For instance, if you love the striking staircase in your home, take a deep dive into inspiration images showcasing staircases highlighted by colorful stair runners, oversize light fixtures that accentuate their unique beauty, or stunning, eye-catching banisters.

Beware of Trends and Trendsetters

While it can be fun (and almost unavoidable) to keep up with what design elements and interior designers are currently "in," approach trends and trendsetters with caution. Relying too heavily on popular styles, colors, or materials for inspiration will stifle creativity and result in a home that feels outdated quickly. This caution also applies to gathering all your inspiration images from a single designer. Your distinct perspective is what breathes life into your home; relying solely on one (or two) designer's work as a reference will result in a space that feels imitative instead of designed.

Take Notes/Look for Patterns

When you are finished collecting inspiration, pause to review. Reflect on why you saved each image; was it the overall feeling of the space, or a specific detail? You might find some that don't quite align with the rest of your inspiration or that no longer resonate with you—you might not even remember why you saved some of the images in the first place. Feel secure in removing these images to eliminate visual noise and keep your design narrative consistent. Observe any patterns that emerge from the images you saved and make note of elements you were consistently drawn to. The goal here is to identify a throughline of your images to help crystallize a design concept. Your notes should be specific and detailed, as they'll become a critical tool as you are working through your design. Revisiting your notes (rather than the images themselves) will minimize the risk of inadvertently copying a design; this approach grants you more creative freedom in your interpretation of the spaces that informed your style.

Define Your Design Concept

Use the patterns from your mood boards to guide your design concept. Think of your design concept as a word, a phrase, or an elevator pitch for the look you're aiming to achieve. One example could be "eclectic bohemian," in which case your concept might merge elements from different countries and time periods. It could include a multitude of vibrant patterns, textures, and colors to create a well-traveled feeling in your home.

Don't be intimidated by this rule: you get to decide what the concept is; whatever you decide is right. It's meant to establish the framework for all decision-making during the design process and helps ensure your choices work together to achieve a cohesive, deliberate result. Adhering to your design concept is critical in designing a space with a strong point of view and a clear perspective. While specific elements of your design will naturally evolve over the course of your project, it's important that your overarching design concept remains consistent.

A design concept is not a theme. Suppose your design concept is "modern mountain lodge." A common pitfall would be to unintentionally exaggerate this concept. Your instinct might be to integrate antler chandeliers or buffalo plaid into your design, but being too literal in your interpretation of a concept can feel overtly kitschy. While campy designs can be fun and chic, if this isn't your intended outcome, consider incorporating more subtle hints from your concept instead. Perhaps in your modern mountain lodge, you specify millwork built from indigenous trees, or draw color inspiration from native flowers.

Choose Keywords to Tell a Story

This one is a bit of an interior designer cliché, but much of design really *is* about the art of storytelling. Design language can be a valuable tool; the terminology doesn't need to be pretentious or scholarly—it just needs to make sense to you. For example, if you are focusing on your dining room, list three adjectives you would use to describe the ambiance you hope to achieve. Within your "elevated rustic" design concept, perhaps you want the dining room to feel "warm, textural, and organic." Could you apply these three words to the table you're considering? How about the chairs? As you work through your project, revisit your keywords to maintain consistency and prevent inadvertent deviation from your storyline.

Purge Items That No Longer Serve You

Removing furniture or decor pieces from your home can sometimes be as impactful as adding new ones. There's a quote I love by celebrated designer William Morris: "Have nothing in your house that you do not know to be useful or believe to be beautiful." In other words, when an item in your home no longer aligns with your design concept, it's time to sell or donate it. You can find many services available to help you with this: Facebook Marketplace, Craigslist, AptDeco, Chairish, or auction houses are a few examples. Depending on your location, some services can arrange to pick up your furniture for donation. If discarding a piece of furniture seems to be the best option, you can call your city to arrange a large pick up. Alternatively, you can hire a service like 1-800-Got-Junk? to come into your home and remove unwanted items. One note of caution— avoid being too quick to get rid of too many items; replacing furniture can be wasteful and expensive. Ask yourself if the item you're considering donating can be repaired or refurbished. Before you get rid of something, try using it in another area of your home first as sometimes context makes all the difference. If the piece still doesn't work, it's probably time to say goodbye.

Take Inventory

After combing through your belongings, you'll almost always find items you already own that you wish to integrate into your new design. Measure all the pieces you intend to keep so you can incorporate them into your plans. Take pictures of these existing pieces to include in your schemes (see Rule #32), as you'll want to visualize how they interact with new additions you're bringing into your space. Consider reupholstering, repainting, or replacing hardware on the pieces that you already own. These updates can breathe new life into your existing furniture to help them blend more seamlessly with your new design. It is worth noting that refurbishing or recovering furniture can sometimes be quite expensive, so, while it offers the advantage of creating a personalized look and is an opportunity to refresh sentimental pieces, it's not necessarily always the most cost-effective route.

Assess How You Live

In interior designer Rita Konig's online Create Academy course "Ultimate Guide to Interior Design," she says "luxury means having everything you need within arm's reach." I love this quote because you can interpret it literally when organizing a floor plan (see Rule #17) or a bit more metaphorically to mean a home is most luxurious when its function is optimized for your needs. A white linen down sofa might feel physically delightful to sink into, but it is the opposite of luxury if you have little kids or pets living in your home and the durability of a delicate sofa is causing you stress. Think about how you intend to use your space. Do you love to entertain? Plan to have a lot of long-term visitors? Would hidden storage be a benefit? Is there anything specific you'd love to showcase? Do you work from home? Ask yourself questions like do I want this space to feel formal or informal? What time of day am I most likely to use this room? What activities would I like to take place here? Keeping such questions in mind as you approach different design choices will offer valuable guidance in what material and furniture selections will create the most practical and therefore luxurious environment for you personally.

Make a Shopping List

Once you've solidified how you want your space to look and function, and after you've taken inventory, it's time to outline the precise steps you'll need to take to get your home from its current state to your desired outcome. At this stage, I find it helpful to make a detailed spreadsheet (organized by room, if you're working on more than one). This list should include everything you'll need to purchase. This spreadsheet will later correspond with any floor plans or drawings that you have and is called an FF&E (furniture, fixtures, and equipment) schedule. It refers to all the movable items necessary for furnishing and outfitting a space.

The pieces of information I like to include in my Schedules:

ROOM (IF APPLICABLE)	ITEM	VENDOR	ITEM NAME	FINISH	EXPECTED DELIVERY DATE

ORDER NUMBER	TRACKING NUMBER	PRICE	PHOTO	STATUS	NOTES

Fill in the first two columns of the schedule to outline everything you'll need. Remember to include line items for the final touches like accessories and art. Your completed schedule can serve as your shopping list throughout your project. It will become particularly helpful if you plan to make purchases over a longer period of time or if you're collaborating with a few different people. Should you find yourself lost or overwhelmed during the design process, revisiting the framework of your design concept and schedule can serve as a compass to reorient you in the right direction.

Create a Budget

Whether you are embarking on a ground-up build or simply giving a room in your home a minor face lift, the expenses associated with design projects can accumulate quickly. Approaching your project with a well-defined budget will help mitigate overspending or sticker shock. Establish an allowance for each item you include in your Materials Schedule to come up with your overall budget. If you don't know how to estimate a price for any given piece, try browsing a midrange store (like CB2 or West Elm) where you feel comfortable shopping. Include a placeholder from that store as your starting point. Tally all the line items to gain insight into what you should anticipate spending overall.

Don't forget to consider hidden costs. Even in the most well planned and meticulously managed design projects, it's not unusual for the cost of renovating and furnishing a home to exceed initial expectations. Bear in mind there are often hidden costs to the items you are purchasing such as freight, installation fees, framing, or stain-proofing. There are also always possible contingency costs during a renovation, like opening up a wall to find wood rot that needs to be addressed. Be sure you're comfortable spending at least 15 percent more than what your initial budget estimates; if you're not comfortable with this possibility, you might ultimately end up needing to scale back the scope of work.

When to Hire a Designer

An interior designer can provide valuable help for projects of any scale. Some designers are open to consulting on minor adjustments to a space (like helping source pillows for your living room) while others focus exclusively on complete remodels or new build projects. A good designer will collaborate with you to maximize your budget and avoid costly mistakes. While an interior designer's expertise is beneficial at any juncture when you feel the need for assistance, involving a designer at the project's earliest stage is usually best. For large projects that involve other professionals like architects and contractors, bringing the designer on board as soon as possible helps establish a cohesive team from the outset and ensures that your space is being examined from all perspectives.

How to Hire a Designer

There is no better way to find a professional to collaborate with than through word of mouth. If you don't have friends in the area who can recommend the type of professional you are looking to hire, try exploring a local Facebook group for referrals. Local design stores can be a great source of recommendations for interior designers, as they often have relationships with professionals they trust and work with frequently.

If you're looking to hire a team of experts: such as an architect, designer, and builder and you're unsure where to begin, you can start by hiring one team member and asking them for referrals for the other professionals. These trades work together regularly and will often have established relationships with experts with whom they have good working rapport.

You can explore platforms like Instagram and websites like ADPro and The Expert to find designers whose work resonates with you. Remember to consider working with a professional who is not necessarily local to your area; especially post-pandemic, most designers are quite comfortable working remotely. As an example, I am based in New York and am currently collaborating on a project in Massachusetts with an architect based in Michigan. We manage the project through site visits at key milestones combined with more regular Zoom meetings, and rely on the local builder for regular on-site updates.

What to Expect Once You've Hired a Designer

The role of an interior designer is to enhance your living space. While it can be a significant investment, working with a designer is a valuable tool for navigating a renovation, optimizing your space, and making informed decisions.

While everyone's process will be a little different, building a trusting relationship with your designer is key, as they will be coaching you on what to do with what is likely the biggest and most important purchase you'll ever make: your home. Some clients are hesitant to disclose their budget at the outset of a project for fear that they might be enabling excessive spending or that their budget is unreasonably low. However, professionals won't take advantage of or shame you for your budget, and it's a crucial early conversation to ensure everyone's expectations align. So I recommend following Rules #11 and #12 to come up with an informed budget first, and then bringing that to anyone you will be working with.

Different designers have different styles. Some may offer multiple schemes for your space, while others will present a single plan and adjust it based on your feedback. Working with a designer is typically a collaborative process, which ensures that the designer can best meet the needs of you and your family. Some designers will handle everything from selections to procurement to installation (delivering a TV-like "reveal" of your finished space), while others rely on their clients to do more of the legwork. I believe creative collaboration between a homeowner and designer yields the best results, and setting clear expectations of what you hope to gain by working with a designer is essential for the best client-designer experience.

Working with a Contractor

Working with a general contractor has many benefits, especially in a large renovation. The role of a general contractor is to manage and coordinate all the different subcontractors and tradespeople required throughout the process of renovating or building a home. They have experience and expertise in construction including building codes and construction techniques. In my opinion, hiring an organized, experienced contractor is some of the best money you can spend during a renovation.

Don't be penny-wise and pound-foolish; hiring a more expensive contractor to redo the work of the less expensive, less experienced contractor will cost you twice as much, so better to find someone you feel comfortable with at the outset. Always request references. It can also be a good idea to inquire about the possibility of touring some of their completed spaces, particularly when evaluating a builder. Ideally, the project you tour should be similar in scope to your own so that you're comparing apples to apples.

It's important to work with a contractor with whom you can have an open dialogue. If there is anything you are unclear about, you can never ask too many questions or overexplain your concerns. Plans change all the time during renovations so make sure to put everything in writing and tape up the most up-to-date plans in the space to make sure everyone is on the same page. Schedule regular site visits and check-ins so that you understand project milestones and can address questions as they come up.

Make a Floor Plan

Creating a floor plan is a fundamental step in the process of designing any space. It provides a visual representation of your room's layout, dimensions, and architectural features and ensures your vision aligns with the practical realities of your space. The first step in making a floor plan is to accurately measure your room, which is called doing a site survey. Use a measuring tape to record the length of your walls, noting doors, windows, radiators, and any other architectural features your room may have. Annotate your floor plan with the locations of outlets, the height of windows off the floor, and the ceiling height. I like to record these measurements on graph paper with a scaled ruler and then transfer them to Auto-CAD, but you can find some simple tools online like SketchUp and RoomSketcher to draw your floor plans to scale. Remember to notate the dimensions on the plan itself so that you can see how much space you have when you are furniture shopping.

Consider Different Layouts

Get creative when considering furniture arrangements—a room will often require a lot more furniture and accessories than you initially expect. Using a scale ruler, you can make to-scale cutouts of furniture pieces to move around your floor plan, if that's helpful. I believe best practice is to consider a minimum of two floor plans per room; comparison is an excellent tool for exploring possibilities, learning preferences, and making informed decisions. Pushing yourself to come up with multiple layouts also encourages you to think outside the box—and you might just end up with a good idea.

Some rooms have a natural focal point like a fireplace or a window with a beautiful view that can be a jumping-off point for how to lay out your furniture. Create one plan anchoring your furniture around the focal point to make the most of the unique features your space offers, then try a plan that completely ignores the focal point, forcing you to be creative.

Another tactic if you're struggling to envision two layouts for a space is to create one symmetrical and one asymmetrical floor plan. Symmetrical arrangements tend to feel more serene and formal and offer a sense of order while asymmetrical furniture layouts can add visual interest and personality into a space. You can also go back to Rule #10: think about your ideal function for the room and how your floor plan can help support this function for you.

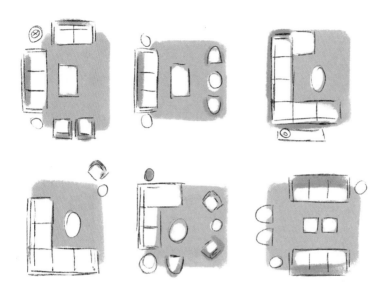

I always like to start my layouts by choosing an appropriate-size rug, as this will anchor and define a specific area in a room. More on this in Rule #45, but in short, ideally the rug will be large enough to fit all the key pieces of furniture completely within its borders. Once you have identified the size of your area rug, position your "hero" piece of furniture (the piece that defines the room—for example, the bed in a bedroom or the sofa in the living room), then plug in the accent furniture to encourage comfortable flow and balance.

Open Floor Plans

An open floor plan is a large area where two or more spaces coexist without any walls dividing them. Typically, these spaces serve shared functions such as a kitchen and a dining room or a combination of a kitchen, dining room, and living room.

When designing a room within an open floor plan, use these tricks:

- **Lighting:** A chandelier centered over a dining table with flush mounts placed strategically over the living area communicates that, while the two spaces are technically in a shared room, their purposes are different.

- **Area Rugs:** Placing a large rug with all the living room furniture on it, for example, clearly delineates that area from the dining space in the same room.

- **Furniture:** Position the back of your sofa toward your dining space to emphasize the separation between your living and dining areas. The rear of a sofa may seem uninviting, so if you opt for this approach, consider incorporating a console table or another low piece of furniture behind the sofa to introduce visual appeal.

Up until the 1940s, American homes traditionally had separate rooms that served specific functions, and the kitchen was almost always toward the back of the house. Open floor plans became popular during the baby boom when casual living began to displace more formal living arrangements and open spaces made it easier for millions of new parents to watch over their growing families. In the post-pandemic era where remote work has usurped traditional office settings, I am seeing a slight shift away from the open floor plan as it can be difficult to work in the same room where kids are playing or someone is cooking a meal. But open floor plans continue to be popular because of the laid-back, social sensibility they lend to a home.

Walkways

Considering how you move through a space is crucial to laying out your furniture. There is a hierarchy of walkways in a home, and each requires a different amount of clearance. "Clearance" as it pertains to a floor plan refers to the unobstructed space needed to ensure comfortable and safe movement. Primary walkways (high-traffic spaces like a main entrance) require at least 36 inches of clearance. Secondary walkways (like the path between the dining room table and a credenza) should be between 24 and 30 inches wide, and if you're laying out furniture in a smaller space or in an area that won't be used frequently, 18 to 24 inches of clearance ensures basic accessibility.

Space Planning for a Small Space

As a designer based in New York City, I have a lot of tricks up my sleeve for making the most of small spaces (see Rule #76). Specifically, as it pertains to creating the best floor plan for a small room; the trick is to incorporate enough furniture pieces that your room feels comfortable and finished, while also employing space-saving techniques.

Think about incorporating multipurpose furniture (see Rule #74) into your plan. Often the temptation when designing a smaller space is to use smaller furniture, but that can make your room feel timid and visually shrink the space further; so, like you would do in any other space—size up if you're between two sizes for an area rug, sofa, or other important item.

Consider including built-in furniture in a small room, like a dining banquette that will eliminate gaps to the walls. A built-in bench in lieu of dining chairs typically saves around 6 inches in a floor plan—a big difference!

Space Planning for a Large Space

When a room is oversize, I like to break it up by creating multiple seating areas or different zones. You can incorporate smaller scale furniture pieces in large rooms by flanking them with sculptural chairs or large potted plants. Moving furniture away from the walls and floating pieces into the center of the room makes seating areas feel more intimate and inviting. This design approach breaks up the vastness of a space, fosters a sense of coziness, and encourages conversation. It also allows you to showcase the furniture from all angles, maximizing the visual appeal of a room. Placing one large area rug beneath various seating arrangements is an effective way to create a sense of cohesion among the separate zones because the rug acts as a unifying element. Furniture pieces that combine and connect multiple seating areas, such as a daybed or a tête-à-tête sofa, can be useful in bridging different zones.

Conversely, you can try the opposite approach and arrange two sofas back-to-back (maybe with a console table between them) to create completely distinct seating areas. In a large space, using two coffee tables instead of one can visually break up the vastness of a single large surface, allowing for more flexibility in arranging tabletop accessories, providing functional surfaces within different seating areas, and creating a more dynamic look.

In a large room it's especially important to layer accessories, art, patterns, textures, books, and decor items to add warmth and character. These details create an inviting atmosphere and make a large room feel cozy and comfortable.

Will It Fit?

A key part of making a successful floor plan is to ensure that larger furniture not only fits in your plan, but that it can also be maneuvered into its intended room. Include measurements of entryways, doorframes, hallways, staircases, and elevators when surveying your space. If you do find yourself in a scenario where you've purchased a piece of furniture that proves challenging to physically place in the designated space, don't panic. You can find a "furniture doctor" service that specializes in disassembling furniture, moving it where it needs to go, and reassembling it. Removing a banister from a staircase or taking doors off their hinges can also help accommodate oversize pieces, while sometimes the solution can be as simple as unscrewing the feet from a piece to get it through the door. These solutions can be helpful in an emergency, but it's far more efficient, cost-effective, and less stressful to avoid these challenges by measuring your entrances and pathways before purchasing your furniture.

What to Bring with You

When shopping for furniture, always bring along your floor plans and your tape measure to ensure the pieces you're considering will fit comfortably within your space and align with your proposed layout. Reviewing your mood board notes before you go shopping can be helpful in keeping you on track with your design concept and remind you of your desired aesthetic and style. Bring along materials you've already selected, such as paint chips or rug swatches, to help you visualize how new pieces will fit within your overall scheme.

Where to Shop

The "Rule of Thirds" in design suggests that your furniture should be one-third vintage, one-third bespoke, and one-third big box. This mix makes your space feel collected and curated and helps to keep your budget under control. Strategically splurging on some special vintage and bespoke pieces elevates the look of the cost-effective big-box purchases.

When it comes to buying your "hero" furniture pieces (see Rule #28) I believe in investing in high-quality pieces you can keep for a lifetime. Do a lot of research and spend time looking for what you really love. Start at high-end stores to see what's available and get inspired, then shop around to find similar pieces within budget. Etsy, Chairish, and 1stDibs are great online resources for pre-loved or bespoke furniture. Part of the fun of decorating is finding items from artisan makers or while you are traveling, and weaving these items into your design will make your home feel personal. Even if you particularly love one store, don't go overboard shopping there—too many pieces from the same place will feel like you're replicating their showroom.

What to Take Home with You

- **Photos:** Taking photos of furniture pieces from various angles while shopping is practical and helpful, as the photos provide a visual record of the items you liked, allowing you to assess them later. This is especially useful if you're visiting multiple stores. Always take a photo of the item's tag, too.

- **Tearsheets:** A tearsheet provides an information summary about a specific piece of furniture. It typically includes images of the item from different angles as well specifications about the piece like dimensions, materials, and pricing. Most high-end stores offer tearsheets, so ask for these when you're browsing.

- **Swatches and Samples:** Swatches let you see how a material will look with your decor and in your home's natural light. For spaces that will host kids, pets, or dining, test the durability of fabric options by deliberately spilling wine or ketchup on a swatch. You can also test swatches of outdoor furniture materials to see how they hold up to the elements, or get samples of wood finish for furniture legs to see how they interact with the rugs, flooring, and other pieces in the space. Be sure to label your swatches and samples (e.g., "arm-chair upholstery").

Receiving Purchases

When you're ready to purchase your materials and furniture pieces, log everything into your schedule (see Rule #11) so you can see your budget is progressing. For our residential projects, we make it a point to obtain pricing for as many components as possible before placing any orders to ensure we stay on budget before incurring any expenses.

Open and inspect items as soon as they are delivered to you, even if you aren't installing them immediately, so you can be aware right away of any potential issues that might impede your project. Identifying issues early is crucial, as it can be difficult to return or exchange items after you've accepted them. This applies to fabric, wallpaper, light fixtures, furniture, and more. If you are sending fabric to an upholsterer, ensure that they inspect the fabric immediately, because once the fabric is applied to your furniture, you're stuck with it. The same goes for wallpaper that has already been cut or applied to a wall.

Update the "status" column in your schedule as soon as items arrive—if your project is a big one, a clear record will prevent any confusion. If you're receiving a lot of materials to your house, consider designating one room as a temporary mail center (many people use their garage for this). Direct all deliveries there and organize them by room so you'll know where to look when you need a specialty lightbulb that arrived months ago.

You can imagine how a new piece of furniture will look in your space, but sometimes people are still surprised once it arrives, kind of like how it takes a few days to get used to a new haircut. Take some time to live with your new item before making any decisions to undo or redo anything. But do confirm the return policy with the vendor so you don't miss your window if you ultimately decide to send it back.

The Sofa

A sofa is not only a significant financial investment in your home but also one of the most frequently used pieces of furniture. Therefore, being an informed sofa shopper is crucial. While there are many factors to consider when choosing the perfect sofa, determining the right size is the best starting point. The "two-thirds rule" suggests that your sofa should be approximately two-thirds the length of your room, and your coffee table should be around two-thirds the length of your sofa. If applying this rule doesn't result in a standard sofa size that fits well within your space, it's usually best to round up to a slightly larger size. Because objects on a floor plan can seem smaller than they do in your actual living space, use blue tape to mark a sofa's dimensions on your floor to see whether the size you're thinking about feels right.

Once you've established the appropriate size for your sofa, the next consideration is its style. There is a wide range of sofa styles, from traditional tufted settees to sleek ultra-modern designs. To make a choice that aligns with your desired mood for the room, remember your design concept and refer to your mood board notes. Since the sofa is a focal point in the living room and greatly influences the overall ambiance, it's essential to choose a style that goes with the vision of the room, and helps to underscore your vision.

A high-quality sofa should last for approximately ten to fifteen years. While some furniture is relatively risk-free to purchase online, a sofa is one of your long-term invesments, so I recommend visiting showrooms to find a comfortable option.

A sofa should strike a balance between feeling soft but also supportive for your back. It should also feel well-padded and relatively firm when

SECTIONAL

TUXEDO

TRADITIONAL

MID-CENTURY MODERN

CHAISE LOUNGE

LOVESEAT

you first purchase it, as the stuffing will inevitably compress and soften over time. Sofas are generally stuffed with either polyurethane foam or a hybrid of foam and feathers. Some high-end sofas are stuffed with 100% down feathers; these require more maintenance because they quickly lose their shape. There isn't a "best" option, but there will likely be an option that feels best for you; so, it's important to understand what you find most comfortable as it will save you time in your search. Squeeze the corner of a sofa arm to make sure you can't feel the wood frame through the stuffing. If you can, the sofa is not well padded; this will only get worse over time.

A high-quality sofa frame will be made of kiln-dried hardwood. Sofas with frames made of particleboard or metal are less expensive, but will be less durable and have a shorter life. A useful test for assessing the strength of a sofa frame is to lift one of the front legs. If the other leg doesn't lift with it and remains on the floor, it may indicate that the sofa's frame is already warped.

Matching the upholstery to the intended usage of the sofa is essential for both practicality and aesthetics. For high-traffic spaces, opt for durable, family-friendly fabrics, like the kinds described in Rule #81. Textured and patterned fabrics conceal stains better than flat solids. Leather is a great choice for spaces with pets because hair and (most) spills can be wiped right off. Slipcovers are practical as they can easily be removed and either machine-washed or dry-cleaned. Indoor-outdoor fabrics repel spills and allow for easy stain removal, so if you have your heart set on a light-colored upholstery these can help ensure durability. While I strongly advocate for the idea that every part of your home should be utilized and enjoyed, you can reserve more precious materials like silk or linen for areas that are designated for adults or where you want to convey a more formal mood.

The Bed and Mattress

The bed serves as the central focal point of the bedroom and plays a critical role in defining the room's mood. Let's start with the bed frame: the most common materials are upholstery, wood, and metal. An upholstered headboard adds a layer of cushion and softness to a space; a wood bed frame appears visually stronger; and a wrought-iron frame adds a vintage touch.

Consider whether you want a low- or high-profile bed frame. A headboard with a lower profile gives the impression of the bed blending into the surroundings, fostering a serene atmosphere, while a taller headboard commands attention and makes a bold statement. In compact bedrooms, a clever design trick is to paint or upholster the headboard in a color that matches the wall, creating a sense of roominess. Also consider how the bed's height will affect the overall look of the room, ease of getting in and out of bed, and your storage needs. If you need extra storage, for instance, a platform bed frame with drawers or bins underneath is a good option.

While mattresses come in standard sizes, bed frames can vary significantly in terms of depth and width of the headboard, footboard, and side rails. Make sure you include the dimensions of the bed frame itself in your floor plan rather than relying on mattress size. Ideally, you want to center your bed so you can fit a nightstand on either side; if this doesn't work on one of your walls, placing a bed in front of a window can look unexpected and beautiful.

While a bed is essential in setting the mood for the space, the mattress is critical in making sure it is comfortable for you. Before purchasing your mattress read about the requirements for your specific bed. Most beds hold a standard 8- to 14-inch-thick mattress but some will require thinner or thicker mattresses; some will also require a box spring while others cannot accommodate them. (If you are using nightstands, make a note of the height of your mattress as the top of your nightstands should fall within 2 inches of your mattress top.)

You'll also want to consider your preferred sleep position and any specific comfort requirements like firmness or support. Different mattresses cater to different sleep styles. If you have allergies or specific health concerns, focus your search on hypoallergenic and antimicrobial mattresses. Here are the most common mattress types:

- **Innerspring:** Best for back and stomach sleepers, these tend to have a firm feel, which can be especially beneficial for those who need more spinal alignment.

- **Memory Foam:** Best for side sleepers and people with pressure-point issues, as memory foam provides support and pressure relief, particularly for the shoulders and hips.

- **Latex:** Best for combinaton sleepers and people with allergies. Latex provides a responsive and supportive surface and is resistant to dust mites and allergens.

- **Pillow-Top:** Great for side sleepers; the extra layer of padding cushions the shoulders and hips and reduces pressure points. And best for people who prefere a softer sleeping surface.

- **Natural Material:** Made from organic and eco-friendly components, these are best for indiviuals who prioritize environmentally friendly products, health-conscious people, and hot sleepers.

It can be helpful to go into a store to test out mattresses, but the best way to make sure a mattress is a fit for you is to try it out at home. Always clarify what the return policy is before buying; many brands will let you keep the mattress for around 100 days. Look for customer reviews to gain insight into performance and durability, paying special attention to feedback from people who mention similar sleep preferences to yours.

Inquire about the warranty on the mattress and what happens if you encounter durability issues. A good mattress should last about eight years, and since the quality of your sleep affects every aspect of your life, investing the time and money to find the best one for your needs is worth it.

A box spring is a wooden frame with springs primarily used to provide a stable, supportive surface for the mattress. It's main functions are to support weight evenly across a mattress, raise the mattress so that it's a more comfortable height on a bed frame, and help absorb transfer of motion from one side of the bed to the other. Box springs have become somewhat less critical as mattress technology has improved but some beds do still require them.

The Dining Table

Dining tables come in all different shapes and sizes; a rectangular dining table is the most traditional and versatile, a round table is chic and conversational, and an oval table feels unexpected and helps soften the lines of an angular room. Dining tables come in all different materials from wood to glass to stone. The shape and style you choose will help set the tone of your dining area.

Think of how many people you want to seat at the table. If you're someone who hosts overnight guests regularly a good rule of thumb is that there should be as many seats at the table as there are beds for your guests to sleep in. Otherwise, think about how many you'll need to

PEDESTAL

TRESTLE

FRENCH COUNTRY

MID-CENTURY MODERN

CONTEMPORARY

FARMHOUSE

seat on a regular basis. Keep in mind that every person needs around 24 inches at a dining table to eat comfortably. With these specs in mind, you can play around with different shapes in your floor plan to see what works best in your space.

Traditional dining table leg styles include pedestal, trestle, and four-legged. The table's leg style will help determine the stability of the table as well as the flexibility of seating arrangements. (You can accommodate more seats around a pedestal table since the absence of legs allows for additional seating to be arranged closely.) If you occasionally host larger gatherings, consider a table with an extension leaf—that way you can expand your table to accommodate more place settings when needed, while keeping the table's footprint more modest day to day. Almost all dining tables are between 28 and 30 inches high, but it can be helpful to test the chairs (especially armchairs) with your table to ensure they fit well when not in use, and that the table height in relation to the chairs makes for comfortable dining.

The Desk

The right desk will support your productivity and help create a comfortable work environment. Determine your specific work requirements by asking yourself questions like: Do you need space for multiple monitors? Do you have a lot of paperwork? Will other people be collaborating or sitting at the desk with you? Or will you be primarily using your desk to catch up on emails and pay bills? Once you've identified how you will use the desk, consider the space it will go in, and the attributes it needs.

The length of your desk should optimize available space in your room so that you have as much surface area and leg space as you can comfortably fit. The height should allow for proper alignment of your computer; you want your arms to rest on your desk at a 90-degree angle. Your monitor should be at eye level so that you aren't straining your neck.

Look for desks with built-in cable management solutions, especially if you have multiple monitors. If you need to store documents or office supplies, choose a desk with drawers. And don't forget to consider how the desk's design, color, and materials fit into your design concept—like every other piece of furniture, a desk contributes to the overall aesthetics of a room.

If you don't have space in your home for a dedicated home office, you'll need to figure out where else in your home you can incorporate a desk. In a living area, consider situating it behind a floating sofa (this will keep you from facing a wall while you are working), opt for a desk style that resembles a console table. Outfitting it with trays and countertop accessories keeps it well-organized and will stop your living space from feeling like an office. If you want to integrate a workspace into your bedroom, try positioning the desk at the foot of your bed or using it as a nightstand. Include an adjustable table lamp on your desk/nightstand so that your workspace gets even lighting and at night you still have cozy reading light.

In cases where your desk is placed in a room with other uses, if possible, try to arrange it in a way that avoids having the back of your monitor facing the door when you enter the room, as this setup doesn't provide the best visual appeal. Flowers and a candle not only enhance the experience of sitting at a desk but also add appealing decor elements when your desk is serving double duty.

Scheming

The process of laying out the photos of your furniture items and your material swatches to evaluate your options is called scheming. It's typically best to start your schemes with the hero piece of furniture as those have the most significant impact on the overall design and function of a space. At this stage, you should experiment with different furniture pieces, fabrics, paint samples, and material swatches to confirm your selections complement each other. You can scheme on a large table, on the floor, or on a pin-board—just be sure you can see all the items you plan to put into any given room at once so that you can easily read how they work together. Try to scheme in the room you're designing so you can see how the materials interact with the natural lighting of the space. Revisit your schemes throughout the day to see how the colors look in different lighting, especially if you're working on a room you will use both day and night. Remember to consider your floor coloring when looking at your swatches (especially paint and rug swatches) since flooring takes up so much surface area in a room.

Use a larger swatch of a fabric that will take up more space in a room, like your sofa upholstery. Place smaller swatches of the pillows you intend to use on this sofa next to it.

Vary, Vary, Vary

Varying silhouettes and proportions help build a layered look in a room. Always include a few different furniture heights in your space. Think of your room as a cityscape; the skyline is a lot more beautiful and interesting to look at when there are distinct heights, colors, and shapes to take in. Layering pieces like stacks of books, plants, lamps, and art will be helpful in moving your eye around the room. If you have a squat sofa maybe you want a lighter, leggier accent chair. Always avoid "sets" of furniture as they look stale and uninspired. While scheming room by room, remember to evaluate your project as a whole to ensure your entire home feels cohesive, especially in open concept spaces or connected rooms.

Mixing and Matching Patterns

Over the years, I've heard feedback from my clients that mixing and matching patterns feels like an intimidating corner of interior design. While there is no set formula, I do have helpful tips you can use to create a balanced, elevated look. If you are incorporating bold colors or patterns into your space, make sure to spread them out throughout the room. One concentration of something loud feels jarring while incorporating bold moments evenly throughout a room moves the eye around and feels interesting.

Stick to your defined color palette and design concept keywords (see Rules #35 and #17, respectively). Then choose a dominant base color that will serve as your "neutral" (even if it's not a neutral color, it will serve as the unifying element in all your patterns). Combining larger-scale patterns (like a wide stripe) with smaller-scale ones (a ditzy floral print) creates contrast and visual interest, and prevents patterns from competing or looking busy. Incorporate more subtle, understated patterns (a small check) to balance out the impact of bolder ones. Textures can act as their own pattern, plus they add a tactile element into your space. Lastly, remember to use solid colors to break up patterns and provide visual relief.

If you want to incorporate pattern but still find yourself concened about achieving the perfect combination, opt for a single print and use it extensively throughout the room. You can apply your chosen pattern to wallpaper, window treatments, upholstery, and lampshades. Using one pattern in this way creates a chic and high-impact look and alleviates the stress of deciding what patterns work together.

Color Schemes and Sample Palettes

Our reactions to colors are visceral and personal, so ultimately, your own taste will determine what colors "go" with others. If you don't know where to begin, color schemes are sets of rules you can use to determine your palette. Mastering these gives you the framework to create color palettes that look professional and sophisticated. There are six kinds of color schemes:

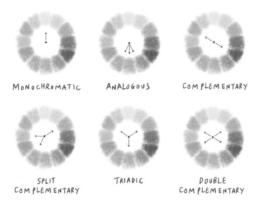

MONOCHROMATIC   ANALOGOUS   COMPLEMENTARY

SPLIT COMPLEMENTARY   TRIADIC   DOUBLE COMPLEMENTARY

- **Monochromatic:** Uses different shades of the same color; for example, navy, royal blue, indigo, and powder blue. These schemes are easy to create and make a space look pulled together and refined.

- **Analogous:** Uses colors next to each other on the color wheel; for example, deep blue, blue-green, and blue-violet. These schemes are soothing to the eye thanks to their subtle variation. An easy approach to incorporating an analogous color scheme is to use one color predominantly and integrate additional colors as smaller accents.

- **Complementary:** Uses two colors directly across from each other on the color wheel; for example, shades of blue and orange. The tension in these color schemes feels intense, so they are not typically used predominately in residential interiors.

- **Split Complementary:** Uses one main color and the colors on each side of its complementary color as accents; for example, blue as the primary color with orange-yellow and red-orange accents. These schemes create a calm, layered mood and appear complex.

- **Triad:** Uses three colors that are equidistant from one another on a color wheel. These work best when one color is the "hero" and the other two play supporting roles; for example, blue as the main color with yellow and red as accents.

- **Tetradric or Double Complementary:** Uses two complementary color schemes next to each other on the wheel. The best way to use them is to select a main color and then use more muted tones of the other three colors; for example, blue as the predominant color with muted shades of orange, red, and green woven throughout the design. These schemes create a rich, vibrant look.

Much like with pattern, dispersing color throughout a room, as opposed to concentrating it in a single area, encourages your eye to explore the space. This has a soothing effect, even when using vibrant colors, because it creates balance. It's important to include neutral colors within your palettes to provide moments of visual reprieve. To ensure your color palette feels balanced, select one color and use it predominantly, then choose a secondary color and use it slightly less. Continue this approach with additional colors, gradually decreasing how much you're using them to keep it from feeling like all the colors are competing for attention.

Color Psychology

Color psychology is the study of how different colors impact our emotions, moods, and overall well-being. Designers use this tool to create specific atmospheres. While associations can vary from culture to culture, use the cheat sheet below to help select the colors that best support the mood you are trying to create in your space.

- **Red:** passion, excitement, high energy
- **Orange:** warmth or overstimulation
- **Yellow:** happiness
- **Green:** nature, freshness, sickliness
- **Blue:** calm, serenity, cleanliness, cold
- **Purple:** luxury, decadence
- **Pink:** sweetness, femininity, vulnerability
- **Brown:** earthiness, heaviness
- **Black:** sophistication, power, mystery
- **White:** purity, cleanliness, sterility
- **Gray:** balance, dullness

I once read an article about a now well-known fast-casual salad chain that was struggling to build its business and so sought the assistance of an external consultant. One prominent finding related to the branding and interior design: the logo and brick-and-mortar spaces featured a yellow-green color that potential customers found off-putting. They replaced it with a rich, fresh-feeling shade of green, which turned out to be pivotal in turning the business around.

How to Choose a Paint Color

When selecting paint colors, consider how the spaces in your home relate to each other and how one room leads to the next, particularly in open concept layouts and/or on the first floor of a home where the rooms tend to be more interconnected.

Think about the room's purpose and what time of day you will predominantly be using that space. Apply paint samples to multiple walls within the room to see how the light interacts with colors from various angles; lighting has an enormous effect on how we perceive color.

In north-facing rooms, where the light tends to be cooler, steer clear of colors with cool undertones to avoid a sterile feel. Southern-exposed rooms receive more warmth and brightness, so these offer greater flexibility in color choice. East-facing rooms are bathed in cool morning light and remain well-lit throughout the day, so use a cooler palate here to complement this. The intense sunset glow in west-facing rooms can be amplified by selecting warm colors. If you are still stumped, Farrow and Ball offers a wonderful in-home or virtual color consultation service to help determine the best paint colors for your space and desired aesthetic.

Finally, remember that paint looks different after it is dry, so never judge a swatch while it's still wet.

Think about what you wish to accentuate or conceal in a room: if you love a special architectural detail, paint it in an accent color to make it stand out; painting an ugly radiator or pipe the same shade as your walls can help it "disappear." Consider introducing bold paint colors in unexpected places, like the interiors of closets or cabinets. This makes a striking impact and adds a fun "pop" when you engage with the space but remains concealed most of the time.

Paint Finishes

Your choice of paint finish affects both aesthetics and durability. Match the finish to your lifestyle, the room's purpose, and your visual preferences to ensure a successful and long-lasting paint job. As a general rule, the higher the sheen, the more imperfections a paint color will show. But here's a rundown of what's available, in order from flattest to shiniest:

- **Flat:** The most matte of the standard finishes. Since this velvety paint finish doesn't reflect any light, it conceals wall imperfections more readily than others, but is typically more difficult to clean. This combination makes it the most popular choice for ceiling paint. Generally speaking, the flatter the paint finish, the less expensive it is. Flatter finishes will also feel physically lighter when you pick up a gallon container of them up because they have fewer (pricey) binders.

- **Eggshell:** Just as it sounds, this finish resembles the subtle reflective quality found on the shell of an egg. It offers a subtle sheen that's easy to clean, making it a popular choice for interior walls.

- **Satin:** The greater sheen of satin paint makes it an excellent choice for wet areas of the home, as it also repels more water. The balance of durability and the fact that it still hides imperfections well also makes this a good choice for homes with pets and children, and for frequently used cabinetry.

- **Semigloss:** It's a sheen right in between satin and high-gloss paint. I typically use semigloss for trim because it subtly highlights architectural features. It's an excellent choice for bathrooms and wet areas because it repels moisture and has anti-mildew properties, as well as for kitchen cabinetry and millwork thanks to its durability and cleanability.

- **High-Gloss:** A specialty finish that makes a striking visual statement, high-gloss reflects the most light, giving it a shiny, liquid-like appearance. The binders in the paint make it highly durable, but it also highlights imperfections, so be sure the surface you are painting is perfectly smooth. This often requires skim-coating or plastering your wall ahead of painting, which is time-consuming and costly.

	The terms "high-gloss" and "lacquer" are used interchangeably, but the former is applied as a complete paint system and is available in various colors, where the latter is a clear topcoat finish applied over existing surfaces to achieve a similar glossy look. While a labor-intensive process, high-gloss painting can be a DIY project, while lacquer is typically sprayed by professionals.

Selecting a Paint Type

In addition to thinking about the color and finish of your paint, it's important to consider the type of paint that best suits your needs. Paints can generally be categorized into two main groups: water-based (latex) and oil-based. Water-based paints are commonly used in residential settings due to their lower chemical content and quicker drying times. Oil-based paints tend to be pricier but offer greater durability, making them an excellent choice for cabinetry and woodwork. Oil-based paints offer a beautifully smooth finish and show fewer brush strokes compared to water-based paints. However, it is worth noting that oil-based paints dry slowly and emit a potent odor, which requires you to vacate your home during the drying process.

Creating a Paint Schedule

After you've made color and finish choices, it's important to document precisely which areas will be painted with which colors and in which finish to eliminate potential confusion and also to serve as an easy reference guide for future touch-ups. Your Paint Schedule should include the following:

ROOM	SURFACE	PAINT BRAND	PAINT COLOR	PAINT FINISH	NOTES

Choosing the Right Wallpaper Type

Traditional wallpaper is crafted from paper of varying thickness and durability; some traditional wallpapers feature a protective coating to enhance longevity. Vinyl, fabric, and textured wallpapers are applied using the same general techniques as traditional paper but offer distinct properties. Vinyl wallpapers possess a resilient, plastic-like hand that facilitates easy cleaning, making them suitable for wet spaces. Fabric and textured wallpapers, like grass cloth or silk papers, come in varying degrees of durability and contribute a rich tactile dimension to your space, introducing texture without the boldness of intricate patterns.

Choosing a Wallpaper Pattern

Wallpaper can have a profound influence on the mood of the space. It's a very impactful way of immersing a space in pattern, color, or texture. One tip for selecting a wallpaper pattern is to scale the pattern of your wallpaper to the scale of your room: small room = small wallpaper print, big room = big wallpaper print. If you have a striking piece of art for a specific room, using a smaller-print wallpaper is often better since it won't compete with the artwork. Buy a single roll of the wallpaper you are considering and pin a strip of it up in your space. Leave it on the wall for a few days to see how you feel about it over time and in different lighting.

Wallpaper has been around since 200 BCE, when the ancient Chinese began adorning their walls with handpainted rice paper. As time progressed, the concept of wallpaper spread to Europe, gradually replacing the earlier practice of decorating walls with hard-to-maintain fabrics. During this period, and all the way up to the Industrial Revolution, wallpaper was reserved for the wealthy, and symbolized means and taste. As with most interior design motifs, early wallpaper designs were elaborate and featured fanciful shapes, or as one of my design professors liked to say, "Earlier is curlier, later is straighter."

In the fifteenth century, block printing replaced hand painting as the primary method for making wallpaper. Block printing involves carving designs onto wooden "blocks" and stamping these designs onto paper. However, despite the fact that block-printed wallpaper was less time-consuming than it's hand-painted predecessors, its production still required manual labor, and thus it remained a luxury item.

The introduction of the printing press and the advent of synthetic dyes made wallpaper more broadly accessible, and also expanded the range of patterns and colors available. Twentieth-century design trends shifted toward cleaner lines, geometric patterns, and abstract motifs. Additionally, advancements in materials led to the development of increased durability and resilience.

Today, the wallpaper industry has evolved further with the integration of digital printing technologies, and the expansion of the range of available wallpaper types, encompassing options like traditional, vinyl, fabric, textured, and peel-and-stick. (See Rule #41.)

Ordering and Hanging Wallpaper

Wallpaper is printed in batches and each batch will be assigned a dye lot. When you order wallpaper, you want it all to come from the same dye lot so that you know it will all match (this is the case with fabric, too). Although hanging wallpaper can be approached as a DIY project, it's generally better to entrust this task to professionals, due to the complexity of the installation and specific considerations for each type of wallpaper. A professional will also help ensure that you order the correct quantity of wallpaper, accounting for repeats in patterns and tricky overage requirements around areas like windows, doors, or cabinetry.

Although modern wallpaper primers and linings have made significant advancements in facilitating a clean and uncomplicated removal process, wallpaper should still be regarded as a semi-permanent alteration to your living space. For a more user-friendly DIY option, try peel-and-stick wallpapers, which offer the advantage of easy removal when you decide to make a change.

Trims and Molding

Adding trim to your walls dresses them up. Trim serves both practical and decorative purposes. You can paint your trim an accent color (often white) to create visual interest or, for a more subtle look, you can paint it the same color as your walls but in a finish with slightly more sheen. Generally speaking, molding is larger and more ornate in traditional designs and simpler and sleeker in more modern designs (earlier is curlier!). There are many kinds of molding, and it is typical to find a few different types in a single room. The most common ones are:

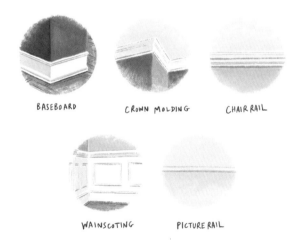

BASEBOARD   CROWN MOLDING   CHAIR RAIL

WAINSCOTING   PICTURE RAIL

- **Baseboards:** Typically installed at the bottom of the walls, where they meet the floor. They serve to protect the wall from damage and provide a finished, polished look. Baseboards help conceal any gaps or unevenness between the wall and the floor.

- **Crown Molding:** Installed where the wall meets the ceiling. It adds elegance and a sense of height to a room, making it appear more finished and grander. Not all rooms have crown molding and adding it can be considered an "upgrade."

- **Chair Rail:** A piece of trim installed horizontally at the height of a chair back. It protects the walls from chair scuffs and marks.

- **Wainscoting:** Typically falls at a similar height on the wall to a chair rail but features decorative panels that go all the way to the floorboards. To make your ceiling appear higher, keep your chair rail and wainscoting on the lower side. The term "wainscoting" includes various styles such as beadboard, board and batten, and shiplap.

- **Picture Rails:** Trim installed around a foot below the ceiling. They are used for hanging artwork without putting nails in the wall.

Feel free to get creative and use molding for your specific needs. In a recent Brooklyn brownstone renovation, we really wanted to add wallpaper in the bedroom but the plaster walls curved into the ceiling, giving us no dedicated "stop" for the wallpaper. We added a picture rails where the wallpaper would end and painted everything above the trim our ceiling color to clearly delineate between the walls and the ceiling.

Flooring Types

Each flooring material has pros and cons. What fits best in a project often depends on factors such as budget, style preferences, room use, and maintenance requirements. Since flooring takes up so much surface area in a home and is costly and disruptive to replace, consider your choices very carefully. Don't try to incorporate more than a few floor materials in your home, as breaking up the flooring room by room feels choppy.

Hardwood floors are classic and timeless, and add warmth and character to a space. They can be repaired and refinished as needed. Popular types of wood include oak, pine, walnut, and ash. Hardwood floors will come in different plank sizes and different "grades." "Character" grade means that you see more knots and variation in the wood, while "select" grade means these traits have been stripped from the wood; select grade is usually more expensive and uniform looking. I like to mix and blend grades of wood (i.e., 70 percent character grade, 30 percent select) to have the richness and cost savings of the character grade without so much detail that the floor knots are distracting. Hardwood floors can be stained in a variety of different colors and each species of wood will show the stain color differently. Test out stain samples the same way you test out paint samples (see Rule #37). Typically, you want to lay wood flooring parallel to the longest wall in a room to make the room feel larger.

Engineered wood floors are made of a thin layer of real wood on top of a composite material. They are more stable than hardwood and less prone to scratching and water damage but can only be refinished once or twice during their lifetime because of their thin top layer. Both hardwood floors and engineered wood floors come in a multitude of species and sizes.

Tile can be a good flooring option and is usually easy to maintain, especially in wet spaces. There are also nearly limitless options when it comes to color, shape, size, finish, price point, etc. (see Rule #60).

Wall-to-wall carpet is soft and comfortable underfoot. It is most typically used in bedrooms but can also add a luxurious dressing-room-like feel to a walk-in closet. Wall-to-wall carpet can be a good strategy for unusually shaped rooms where figuring out the best area rug size is tricky. Carpet also helps with noise reduction because of its excellent sound-absorbing properties.

Concrete floors are popular in homes with a more modern or industrial design. They are durable, can withstand heavy foot traffic, and, as long as they are installed properly, are easy to maintain; otherwise, they are susceptible to cracking as your home shifts. Concrete floors can feel cold and hard underfoot.

Selecting the Best Area Rug Size

Generally speaking, the larger the area rug you use, the larger your space will feel, but specific considerations vary depending on the room you are furnishing. Here are some guidelines:

- **Living Room:** A rule of thumb is that there should be approximately a 24-inch border between the rug and your walls in a living space. In an ideal world, all the legs of your furniture pieces are contained on the rug. If your sofa is against the wall, at least the front two legs of the sofa and any accent chairs should sit on the rug.

- **Dining Room:** Once you already established your dining table size, add 24 inches to all sides of the table to find your ideal rug size.

- **Bedroom:** Your area rug should start a few inches in front of your nightstands and extend to at least the width of your nightstands, although the wider the better. At the foot of your bed the rug should extend at least 18 inches beyond the foot of the bed (or end-of-bed bench if you have one).

- **Runners:** You want 4 to 6 inches on every side of a floor runner whether this be in a hallway, bathroom, or kitchen. The wider your hallway, the wider the margin can be.

Rug Materials

Understanding the properties of various rug materials is essential for determining the best rug for your space and ensuring proper rug maintenance. Many rugs will consist of a blend of a few materials.

- **Wool:** Wool is one of the best materials for area rugs due to its durability, softness, and easy maintenance. During the first six months of use, wool rugs will usually shed; this typically diminishes over time. Regular vacuuming (using a T-shaped non-rotating vacuum head; see Rule #49) can reduce shedding. In the event of a spill, cover the spill with a damp paper towel and allow the paper towel to absorb the liquid. If the stain persists, repeat the process using Woolite instead of water. Wool rugs are not an ideal choice for damp or humid areas because prolonged exposure to water will lead to fading. They're typically considered a higher-end option in terms of pricing.

- **Silk:** Silk rugs have a lustrous appearance and offer a luxurious softness underfoot, but their delicate nature makes them better suited for areas with low foot traffic. Professional cleaning is recommended, but in the event of a spill, clean it up immediately to avoid ruining the rug's delicate fibers, sprinkle water over the affected area, and then immediately dry it with a blow-dryer. Silk is one of the more expensive rug materials.

- **Sisal, Jute, and Abaca:** These natural materials, each made from fibers of a different plant, add texture and an organic feeling to a space. With shedding properties similar to wool, they have a coarse texture underfoot and are sometimes layered beneath softer wool or silk rugs. Sisal is strong and has excellent sound-absorbing properties; jute is the softest and typically the most affordable, and abaca is the most durable. Maintenance involves regular vacuuming and spills can be blotted carefully with a wet paper towel. (Be sure not to use too much water, as it can degrade the rug.) All three are typically budget-friendly options.

- **Cotton:** Cotton rugs have a flat texture and lend a casual, laid-back look to a space. They don't shed and are often machine washable. Due to their easy maintenance, they are a popular choice for entryways, kitchens, and kids' bedrooms. They tend to be very affordable and come in a wide array of colors, styles, and patterns.

- **Synthetic:** "Synthetic" is an all-encompassing term for rugs made of human-made materials like polypropylene or viscose. They are engineered to be durable, but sometimes have a plasticky, artificial feel to them. To deal with spills on synthetic rugs, blot with water. If this doesn't work, try blotting with club soda. These tend to be more cost-effective than their natural counterparts.

Rug Construction

Construction is also a critical factor in understanding what your rug will feel like and how to best take care of it.

- **Tufted:** If a rug is tufted it means that the fibers are pulled through a (usually latex) base, creating little tufts of fiber. Sometimes the fibers are cut to create a soft, plush feel underfoot. Sometimes the fibers are left looped for a tighter weave.

- **Hand-Knotted:** Hand-knotted area rugs are high-end and can take weeks or even months to make. These are typically heirloom quality rugs that will hold up forever.

- **Flatweave:** Flatweave rugs are thin, light, and (not surprisingly) flat. Popular styles are kilims (usually elaborate, bright colored Persian

rugs) and dhurries (a more subtle Indian style). These are easy to clean but can feel a little severe underfoot so it's extra important to use a good rug pad under them. (See Rule #49.)

- **Shag Rugs:** These have a high pile height (see sidebar) and lend a retro feel to a space. Shag rugs feel very soft and cushiony underfoot but can be hard to keep clean and require regular vacuuming. These will usually shed, especially when you first lay them down.

Typically, the flatter the rug the easier it is to clean but the less comfortable it will feel underfoot. When you are choosing a rug for an area near a doorway measure the height of the gap under the door to make sure the rug won't impede it from opening. If you are choosing a rug for under a dining table or desk, make sure the pile is sufficiently low for a chair to glide over it.

- **Flatweave** rugs refer to any pile height under ¼ inch. Sometimes these are used as wall hangings or for upholstery because their lightness makes them flexible and easy to work with.

- **Medium pile** rugs are ¼ to ¾ inch thick. These can be great for walkways or other high-traffic areas because they tend to be durable but will feel softer underfoot than a flatweave.

- **High pile** rugs are anything over ¾ inch high. These are soft underfoot but require more maintenance than medium pile rugs because debris gets caught in the fibers.

Rug Maintenance

Always invest in a rug pad. A rug pad keeps your rug from moving and curling, enhances the experience of walking on it by making it feel more cushiony, and prolongs the life of your rug by protecting it against scraping the hard floor. Rug pads are especially important for rugs with a flatter weave.

When vacuuming your rug, it's better to use a T-shaped non-rotating vacuum head because heads with rotating brushes will pull at the fibers in your rug, leading to increased shedding. (If your rug has tassels, do not vacuum them, as they will pull and damage your rug.)

Have all rugs professionally cleaned every few years. Even with regular vacuuming, dirt can hide within rug fibers so having them treated will prolong the life of the rug.

Rotate your rugs every once in a while to distribute wear and exposure evenly; this is especially important for a rug that is placed in a very sunny area, as the sun can fade the colors. If your rug is small enough, take the opportunity to hang it out the window and beat it (imagine like grandmas in old movies do). You'll be shocked to see how much dirt and dust comes out of even the most meticulously cared for area rug. While you're moving your rug, vacuum the back of it and clean the floor beneath it to reduce debris buildup.

For material-specific tips on maintaining your rugs, see Rule #47.

Down Lights

Using a combination of light sources gives you greater control over the way a space feels and functions. To boil it down: down lighting (overhead lights) gives better function, while up lighting (most lamps and sconces) creates more of a mood.

The debate about where and whether to include overhead lighting is controversial in the interior design world. Overhead lighting can be in the form of recessed lighting, flush mount fixtures, or a statement light, like a chandelier.

Most designers I know dislike recessed lights because they can be unslightly on a ceiling and don't provide a flattering glow. Trends in

recessed lights, especially relating to their size, tend to change rapidly, so they can date a space. If you do incorporate these lights, I recommend putting them on a dimmer so you can have greater control over the brightness and mood they provide. In fact, I recommend putting all overhead lighting on a dimmer for that very reason.

I like to use a series of the same flush mount fixtures overhead because the repetition pulls your eye through the space to make it feel cohesive. If there's an area you want to highlight (think an extra-high ceiling) or a space you want to define (like a dining area), a statement light fixture might be an opportunity for you to incorporate something sculptural and architectural.

To make a big impact with overhead lighting consider playing with scale or introducing a colorful fixture. Using a round chandelier above a rectangular dining table is an unexpected way to introduce a new shape into your scheme. Chandeliers and pendant lights can be a good place to incorporate more delicate materials (particularly in a home with kids or pets), as they are out of reach and difficult to damage.

In terms of how high you should hang overhead lighting, you typically want at least 8 feet of clearance for walking space. Chandeliers should hang around 30 to 36 inches above your dining table, but this measurement will vary depending on your ceiling height (the higher the ceiling, the higher the fixture should hang). The same rule of thumb goes for pendants over a kitchen island.

Under-cabinet lighting illuminates the worktop in your kitchen and doesn't cast a shadow on your workspace. I like to install outlets on the underside of cabinets next to the LED lighting so that backsplashes aren't broken up by unsightly outlets.

Up Lights

If bright overhead lights are for functional dinner-party cleanup, the sexy mood that floor lamps, table lamps, and sconces provide is for crafting the vibe of the party itself. Up lighting drenches a room in a warm, beautiful glow and creates a cozy atmosphere.

Up lighting also offers some decorative possibilities; a colorful, patterned lampshade can liven up a room and can refresh a simple lamp you already own. You can buy these lampshades ready-made, or there are Etsy vendors who will custom-make them in a fabric of your choice, if you're looking for something more bespoke.

Including up lights like table lamps or picture lights in a kitchen or on top of a bar makes the space feel more like a warm extension of the home rather than a utilitarian workspace.

Sconces (or wall lights) are generally easier to install than overhead lighting and many companies offer plug-in versions of their sconces to make them renter-friendly.

Sconces with table lamps next to your bed looks layered and gives more optionality for full brightness or soft reading light. If you add sconces near your bed, make sure that the switch is either built into the light itself or add an extra switch near your bed so that you don't need to get out of bed every time you want to use them. Sconces should be no more than a foot away from the side of your bed and around 30 inches from the top of your mattress for optimum comfortable reading light. If you want to add an additional switch near the door for the sconces but don't want to open the walls, you can buy inexpensive wireless light remotes from Lutron.

In keeping with Rita Konig's "luxury means having everything you need within arm's reach" (see Rule #10), at least one lamp should be reachable from your sofa, lounge chair, or bed so you can always adjust your reading light without getting up.

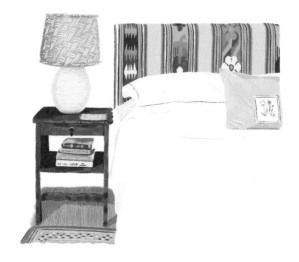

Window Treatment Types

Installing window treatments is always one of the biggest and most rewarding glow-up moments in a project. People often mention natural light as one of the primary reasons they were initially drawn to their home—window treatments highlight that asset, and bring what comes in through the window into your overall design.

A room might have multiple types and sizes of windows, and as long as you use the same fabric for all the windows in a single room, it's okay to mix and match styles to cater to each individual window's properties. For instance, if you have a room with both a bay window and standard windows, it might make sense to do roman shades (see page 80) on the standard windows and use drapery (see below) to highlight the bay window.

The most common window treatment styles are:

- **Drapery:** Drapery feels fancy and lends a sense of drama to a space; it also tends to be one of the more expensive styles of window treatments because it requires a lot of fabric. When hanging drapes, each panel should extend a few inches on either side of the window. There are two benefits of this: it makes your window appear a little bit wider and blocks less of your view. Functionally, drapes are great for light blockage because the edges of your window are always fully covered. You can use a decorative valance (a fabric wrapped board mounted above the window to conceal hardware) if you're looking for a more traditional or whimsical look, or a ceiling-mounted track for something cleaner. My favorite way to hang drapery is to use a classic rod with decorative finials as these add a little something something.

DRAPERY   ROMAN   ROLLER

- **Roman Shades:** Roman shades allow you to choose a decorative fabric and add a splash of personality in a slightly more subtle way than drapery panels. They are a good option for blocking light and a very good option for a window with something beneath it (like a radiator, millwork, or desk), since they stop at the bottom of the window instead of at the floor. You can also use a valance (see page 79) on roman shades to dress them up a bit. Choose flat panel romans with the bottom of the fabric parallel to the bottom of the window or, for a more traditional look, relaxed romans, which curve down at the bottom. This curve is called a belly—cute!

- **Roller Shades:** Roller shades are usually a more cost-effective option as compared to drapery or romans, and they offer a stream-lined look, which can also be layered under decorative window treatment like romans or drapery. Rollers are often made from a plastic material but can also be made from wood or bamboo (also known as matchstick shades) or other durable fabrics. As the name implies, roller shades roll up to the top of your window, so they take up very little space and block very little of a view. Using an easy-to-operate roller shade lends a casual, vernacular sense to a room, even if it's not overly decorative.

- **Shutters:** Like exterior shutters, interior shutters are (usually) made from wood and serve to add privacy and light control. They are a tailored, classic window solution that can be painted in any color, and typically make a room feel more traditional.

- **Wooden Blinds:** Wooden blinds (as the name implies) are made from small pieces of wood and were originally used to keep rooms cooler in hot climates. Chik blinds are similar but are made of bamboo and feature a lattice pattern. These window treatments add a textural and eclectic element to a room and are sometimes layered with drapery.

- **Café Curtains:** Café curtains are small, usually light-weight, drapery panels that cover only the bottom half of a window and end at the windowsill. These offer privacy while still letting light in. They lend an easy-breezy, charming feel to a space.

You may find you want to add privacy without adding a traditional window treatment. Perhaps you are working with a wet space (like a shower), or are in a rental that won't allow you to hard-mount anything, or want to obscure something unsightly outside (like a too-close neighbor). Consider etched glass, an affordable appliqué you can add to an existing window; a piece of stained glass or some stained-glass art hanging in front of the window itself; or taller plants, either in a window box outside or on a windowsill inside.

Hanging Window Treatments

Drapery should always be hung as close to the ceiling as possible to trick your eye into thinking that your window is taller than it is. Panels should at least skim the ground or they will have the same awkward effect as a pair of pants that are just a little bit too short. They can also puddle on the floor for a more dramatic, romantic look. If your floors are uneven, "puddling" can help disguise this. On the flip side, because puddling means your fabric is literally laying on the floor, this style does require more regular maintenance and cleaning.

Window treatments (with the exception of drapery) can be hung from the outside of the window frame, or, if the depth of the frame allows, from the inside. As the name implies, outside mount shades are mounted outside of the window frame. These offer better light blockage and visually elongate your windows; they also block less of the view, because when rolled up they can hang above the window glass. If windows in your room start at different heights, hanging outside-mount roman shades at equal heights can help mask this. The downside of outside-mount shades is that if your window frames have special decorative trim, the shades will cover it.

Conversely, the pros of inside mount shades are that you won't cover any of your window trim. They are also sometimes easier to install because they fit right into the frame of your window. But they require more space in the window frame itself, so depending on the weight of the fabric you are using and the size of the hardware, you may or may not have enough depth inside the frame of your window to be an option.

Choose Bold Moments Strategically

Most people don't want to do major renovations more than once every ten to fifteen years, at most. Staying away from trends when you select your hard build materials like tile and plumbing fixtures and opting for classic materials and silhouettes gives your space longevity.

When you want to make a bold statement, do it with paint color, wallpaper, or other design elements that are more easily updated. Reupholster chairs or a sofa to add new color or pattern to your space. Assuming your kitchen cabinets are hardwood, you can repaint them or replace their hardware. Incorporating accessories and art into your designs (even in a kitchen or a bathroom) make spaces feel personal and warm, but are easy to switch out when you decide to do a refresh. That being said, don't hold back on your design for fear of growing tired of exciting elements. A dull space is likely to become tiresome more quickly than a sofa with unique upholstery or an unexpected kitchen cabinet color that makes your home feel special and personal.

Mixing Metals

Trendy metal finishes—think rose gold or polished brass—can quickly date a space. Replacing them can be challenging since they are often incorporated into plumbing or lighting fixtures. Unlacquered brass and polished nickel are timeless and enduring. But if you have your heart set on using a trendier finish, mixing metals can give your fixtures a more timeless quality because you aren't adhering to what was popular at any given time.

Be sure metals on the same plane match in finish with only one area featuring a contrast. For example, your vanity hardware might be bronze, then your taps can be brass, but your mirror and sconce should revert to the bronze finish you used for your hardware.

When I mix metals, I like to combine cool and warm tones to ensure they're distinct enough to make the mismatched appearance look deliberate.

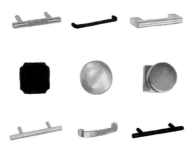

Embrace Patina and Living Materials

Invest in materials and furniture that improve as they wear in. Shiny, sterile materials that are meant to look like a brand-new purchase will not maintain their freshness forever, and instead date your space as they show signs of aging. Organic materials will evolve with their environment and (in my opinion) look better over time. Look for natural stone (see also Rule #64), unlacquered brass, solid wood, copper, terra-cotta, concrete, and other materials that weather gracefully. The same principle applies to furniture pieces and textiles. An overstuffed club chair gains character as its leather gradually softens; a reclaimed wood table carries a history; and an antique rug that is older than the home itself makes guessing the date of the design project impossible. When your furniture and materials aren't frozen in time, the look and feel of your room won't be either.

Avoid Built-In Tech

Trends in styles, sizes, and profiles for recessed lights, AV, and "smart" features change constantly; these are hard to update, so they can quickly date a house. Instead, opt for free-standing AV equipment and smart features that you can update easily as technology advances.

Construction Timelines

When you are working on a renovation, it's crucial to map out lead times for material deliveries to make sure you have everything you need when you're going to need it. Ideally, you should have everything on-site before you start your project so you aren't stuck without a functioning kitchen or bathroom while waiting for pieces to arrive. Give yourself a timeline cushion for the overall project (30 percent longer than the proposed schedule) as renovations often take longer than initial estimates.

Choosing Hard Build Materials

Kitchens and bathrooms require special considerations because they are "wet" spaces. You can obtain samples of tile, stone, and metal just like you can for any soft finishes, so scheming (see Rule #32) for a bathroom or kitchen works largely the same way as scheming for any other space in your home. Make sure to assess your materials together in different lights and test their durability.

Bathroom and kitchen floors need to strike a balance between beauty and functionality. I love the warm, lived-in look of wood flooring, but engineered wood (see Rule #45) has higher durability and thus requires less maintenance, so it could be a better choice for one of these spaces.

Overall, tile is the most practical choice for a bathroom floor, as it's the most waterproof. Matte mosaic tiles have the most grip to them because there are so many grout lines, while large glossy tiles tend to be the most slippery. (Slipperiness is especially important when you are selecting tile for the floor of a walk-in shower or designing a space for someone with mobility challenges.) See Rule #60 for more on bathroom tile.

If you want to make a walk-in shower look larger, try using the same tile for the wall and floor, which will create the look of a single, unbroken space; penny tile (small, round mosaic tiles that are typically the size of a penny); or 4 × 4-inch squares can be especially successful for creating this effect. If you opt to use a different tile on the wall than on the floor, make sure the tiles are different sizes so they don't compete with each other.

You can also use wallpaper and/or wainscoting in a bathroom to give more texture and personality. While vinyl wallpaper (see Rule #41) is the most water-resistant wallpaper material, its plastic texture can be unappealing. If your bathroom is properly ventilated, most traditional

wallpapers will be fine. For a more cozy ambiance, wainscoting (panels applied to a wall for decorative or protective purposes) is an excellent way to add texture. When installing any trim in your bathroom, the typical guideline is to install it 32 inches above the floor, but to make your ceilings appear a little bit higher, you can opt for a slightly lower placement. I like to stop the wainscoting a few inches lower than one-third of the ceiling height. Consider using MDF (medium-density fiberboard, an engineered material) instead of wood, so the trim will not be susceptible to steam-induced warping.

To revisit Rule #38: Because bathrooms are damp, when you are considering paints types, it's important to choose a durable paint that will not get moldy. I almost always use a satin finish on all bathroom surfaces for that very reason.

Tile Decoded

I like to begin a bathroom design by choosing tile, because they usually take up the most surface area. Not all tiles can be used on a floor, in a wet space, with radiant heating, or with other conditions particular to a bathroom. Once you've selected your tiles, send the information to your contractor (if you're working with one) so they can tell you how much overage they need (usually 15 percent) and account for different tile thicknesses to make your surfaces uniform.

Tiles can be made from natural or synthetic materials. The most common for residential bathroom tiles are:

- **Ceramic:** These tiles are durable and often the most affordable option, which makes them extremely popular. Ceramic tiles are typically solid in colors and will have a subtle, coarse feel if not glazed.

- **Porcelain:** At first glance, it can be difficult to tell the difference between ceramic and porcelain tiles, but porcelain tiles are denser and are heavier and more durable than their ceramic counterparts. Their sealed surface makes them almost impervious to water and heat. Porcelain tile can be slippery due to the polished surface, so use smaller porcelain tiles for floors—the grout will help break up the smooth surface. Porcelain tiles tend to be more expensive than ceramic.

- **Natural Stone:** Tiles made from natural stone—such as marble, slate, or limestone—range in look and durability. The fact that they come from nature ensures that no two are the same, and will require a bit of maintenance. They are also generally more expensive than other options.

- **Encaustic/Cement:** These tiles usually have a lot of color and pattern to them, and the designs look "painted on," making them a fun choice for a bolder space. These are prone to staining and require regular sealing and maintenance. Depending on the intricacy of the design these tiles vary greatly in price.

- **Zellige Tiles:** From Morocco, these handmade ceramics feature a glossy glaze in an array of rich colors and have gained popularity in recent years. While you'll often see these in 4 × 4-inch squares, they can come in all shapes and sizes. No two are exactly alike.

Also keep in mind that anywhere that your tile edge is exposed, you'll need to cap the tile, meaning finish the edge, so the unfinished edge isn't visible. Some tiles come with finished edge pieces or special bullnose pieces, and for some you can order coordinating quarter rounds or pencil trims. With proper wall-plane planning, you can even recess your tiles so that the edge bleeds directly into the wall. Metal trim pieces called Schluter strips can be used to cap tile, but these can break up a design and feel like an afterthought.

All About Grout

While grout might not be the sexiest part of your bathroom refresh, it can dramatically improve or detract from the look and longevity of your design. Grout comes sanded or unsanded, but sanded is almost always the better choice; unsanded grout doesn't hold up as well and is usually only used for extremely thin grout lines and scratchable, fragile materials like glass tile. Sanded grout should always be sealed; unsanded grout can go either way. Be sure to read the application instructions on the product you are using.

The width of the grout lines between tiles plays a big role in the overall look of the tile installation. The trend today is for grout lines to be as small as possible to emphasize the tile over the grout. However, handmade tiles have a lot of variation, so you'll need a slightly larger grout line to mask irregularities. One popular look is to choose a grout color that matches your tile so the grout "disappears" and your surface looks more uniform; it can be hard to get an exact match, so look at physical grout samples from the hardware store alongside your tile if you go this route. If you are trying to highlight the shape of your tile, a contrasting grout color makes the shape pop.

Grout darkens and stains over time, and needs to be sealed after installation and again every few years. White grout tends to stain quickly; I prefer to opt for a light silvery color when trying to achieve an overall light look. If you want to update your bathroom without a full renovation, try regrouting to instantly make the space feel cleaner and newer.

Bathroom Hardware and Finishing Touches

- **Bath Towels:** I find towel hooks to be an easier user experience than bars because a hook doesn't require a perfect fold like a towel bar does. If you choose towel hooks, the rule of thumb is to hang them 65 to 70 inches above the floor and within reach of your shower. If you are hanging multiple hooks, aim to have these 6 to 10 inches apart from each other. If you plan to add a robe hook onto the back of your door, mount it at the same height as your other hooks. If you do want to use a towel bar, these are typically mounted around 48 inches off the floor.

- **Toilet Paper Holder:** A toilet paper holder should be mounted 26 inches from the floor and around a foot in front of your toilet bowl.

- **Hand Towels:** A towel ring or bar near the sink should be within a few inches of your sink; height-wise you want to make sure the end of your hand towel lands 2 to 4 inches above your sink's countertop.

- **Hardware Style:** Hardware doesn't need to be from the same set as your plumbing fixtures but should be the same design language; this could be a good place to add in a contrasting material like jute, leather, or porcelain.

- **Shower Curtains/Enclosures:** You can use a shower curtain or have a glass enclosure for your shower. A shower curtain will be more cost effective, and can be a fun place to add color and pattern. A glass enclosure is a higher-end look and should better

protect against water seeping out of the shower into the rest of the bathroom. If you have your heart set on a glass enclosure but don't have the budget (shower glass is something my clients almost universally have sticker shock on), you can easily add one down the road. (In this case, use a tension rod for your shower curtain so it's easy to remove when you're ready to upgrade to glass.)

Glass shower enclosures come in many different styles, but the main two options are doors or stationary fixed panels. You generally need around 30 inches of clearance for a swinging shower door. If you don't have the space, a stationary piece of glass with a 24-inch opening is the rule of thumb for how much space you want to pass through in your shower without risking your bathroom getting totally soaked. You'll also need to decide if you want to do framed or frameless glass. Frameless glass is a cleaner look while framed glass can add a nice design detail, especially in a more traditional space. Make sure you leave space at the top of your shower to let steam out unless you are doing a steam shower in which case you will want to trap all the steam into the space. (If you're doing a steam shower, you also need to make sure to tile the ceiling of the shower so that the extra moisture doesn't make your space moldy.)

- **Shower Benches:** A shower bench is a nice touch; it can be built from stone or tile, or you can purchase a teak (or another wet-friendly wood) bench. If adding a built-in bench, make sure your contractor knows this from the beginning of the renovation so they can properly frame it.

- **Accessories:** Whenever possible, I like to remove bath products from their packaging and store them in decorative canisters instead. A budget-friendly wood shelf or a cute stool next to your tub to store things like bath salts and a loofah can make your bathroom feel luxurious. A candle and a fresh stack of soft towels also help create a serene ambiance. A vintage mirror or something decorative found in a furniture store can be a cozy touch rather than a medicine cabinet. Similarly, consider using a small area rug or runner in lieu of a traditional bath mat. If you don't have your heart set on a particular towel style, classic white (like you'd find in a hotel) always feels fresh and luxurious and is a particularly attractive choice in a guest bathroom because it conveys a sense of freshness.

Kitchen Layouts: Form and Function

There is a rule in kitchen design known as the Magic Triangle, which states that your main three work zones—fridge, sink, and stove—should be configured in a triangle with each side of the triangle between 4 and 9 feet apart. While this doesn't work in every space, it is a nice guide to keep in mind when planning out your kitchen, and the placement of your appliances.

Here are four classic layouts that can serve as a guide to laying out your own kitchen:

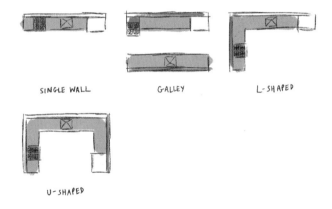

SINGLE WALL   GALLEY   L-SHAPED

U-SHAPED

- The **single-wall kitchen** is best in a small space. In this layout, all appliances are lined up on one wall, taking up minimal floor space, but the resulting lack of counter and cabinet space can make them less efficient. It's not possible to use the Magic Triangle in this configuration.

- A **galley kitchen** is a kitchen in which your appliances are lined up on either side of a hall-like space with a walkway between. These are also good choices for compact spaces, but are generally more efficient than one-wall kitchens because you have more counter space. The downside is it's tricky for more than one person to be in a galley kitchen at once because of the small alley. One trick I like to use in a galley kitchen is to install polished tile on all the walls because the light bounces around the space, which makes it appear brighter. I also like to use the backsplash tile above cabinets because it accentuates height and makes the kitchen appear grander.

- **L-shaped kitchens** have appliances on two adjacent walls; these are very functional because you generally have more counter and cabinet space, and room in the middle to add an island or table.

- **U-shaped kitchens** spread appliances out on three adjacent walls with a large opening in the middle for a walkway, island, or dining table. These require the most space, but also have the most options for counter space and allow multiple people to use the kitchen at once.

No matter the size or configuration of your kitchen, it should feel like a layered, warm space. Antique or vintage dining tables can add that element. Don't be shy about incorporating art like you would in any other room. Wall-mounted plates can add a charming touch, as can a small painting leaning on your countertop. If you include a rug or runner, be sure it is low pile and easy to clean. Accessories like copper pans or te kettles, linen dish towels, and beautiful containers make it feel personal.

Stone Guide

Countertop materials are another a controversial topic in the interior design community. There are so many opinions about what stone is the most practical, most beautiful, most timeless countertop material. Generally, countertop materials can be broken into two categories: engineered and natural stone. Stone slabs generally come in two different thicknesses; 3 centimeters is better for countertops because it can hold more weight, while 2 centimeters is better for vertical surfaces (like a backsplash) because it is lighter.

Synthetic (aka engineered) stone, like quartz, is more durable than natural stone because it is nonporous. It comes in many different patterns (some resembling natural stone), as well as solid colors. While you won't have an issue with spills or stains, heat will burn the resins in synthetic stone, causing discoloration. Synthetic countertops are lower maintenance and less expensive than natural stone countertops. I personally dislike using artificial products designed to mimic natural ones, like quartz with marble-like veining. If a project or client calls for a man-made material, I find it more appealing to choose a solid-color material that embraces what it actually is.

When it comes to natural stone, there are myriad different kinds, but the most popular ones for countertops are marble, granite, and quartzite. Each of these is available in three finishes: polished (shiny), honed (matte), or leathered (matte but with texture that feels like leather).

- **Marble** is a classic, beautiful countertop choice. There are many kinds of marble, ranging from almost solid white to vivid colors with extravagant veining. As a rule, marble is a living material that will require regular sealing and possible refinishing. It is susceptible to water stains, scratching, and etching.

- **Granite** also comes in many different colors; it has a signature ice cream–like texture because it is made of crystallized minerals. Granite is tougher than marble in that it will not stain as easily, although it is still susceptible to heat damage.

- **Quartzite** has become a popular choice in recent years because it resembles marble but is a lot tougher.

Natural stone requires more maintenance than human-made stone and will inevitably show wear and tear. It's similar to having a hardwood floor: You don't choose it because it's low maintenance. You will want to seal natural stone after it's installed and every few years after that. Be mindful of cleaning spills when they happen, especially acidic spills, such as those from citrus.

Many designers (myself included) will argue that the patina of a worn stone countertop makes your space appear more storied and beautiful; in my opinion, when slabs stain, the stain adds warmth and character to a room. So, when your friends warn you against natural stone because it's going to stain, they are right! It's not going to look brand-new except for when it is brand-new, but that's the magic of it. If and when your counters get stained to a point where you're no longer comfortable with it, professionals can refinish the surface for you (again, similar to a wood floor).

The last choice you'll need to make when deciding on your countertop is the profile. Eased edge is the default countertop profile and is just a rounded corner at each edge. Ogee edges are more fanciful and traditional

and feature a bevel at the top of the counter. On the opposite side of the spectrum are square-edge countertops, which have 90-degree corners; these can be sharp if you bump into them and should be avoided if you have kids running around your house.

Don't be afraid to mix your countertop materials in a kitchen. Using a harder working surface on your island and a more delicate slab on the surrounding cabinets can be a good way to add visual interest, while making your primary workspace more durable.

Honor Personal Preferences

Almost every design project requires some level of budget-related compromise. Sometimes due to budgeting constraints you'll need to choose between something that looks exactly as you want it to or that functions exactly as you imagined. When faced with this scenario for an item you'll rarely use, my recommendation is to prioritize aesthetics. Something that looks "off" will bother you every time you see it, whereas if the functionality of an item is compromised it will only pose an issue while you're actively using it. Always prioritize function when dealing with something you'll use regularly.

During a kitchen renovation project in a New York City pied-à-terre, the family was dealing with space limitations, so we hoped to design symmetrical cabinetry around the range featuring three small drawers on either side to make the space appear a bit larger (see Rule #21). We had planned a pull-out spice cabinet with faux drawer fronts on the right side of the range to match the stack of drawers on the left, but the faux fronts turned out to be very expensive. Given that the apartment is not my clients' main residence, and they seldom use the space for cooking, we couldn't justify the cost. We prioritized the aesthetics of matching drawers, with spices stored in another nearby cabinet instead. Had my clients been regularly cooking in this kitchen, we would have taken the opposite approach.

Design Is a Marathon, Not a Sprint

Another approach to addressing budget constraints is to tackle projects in phases. If there's something you've always dreamed of having in your home that's super pricey, it may make sense to implement that splurge item as its own separate project. During a renovation of a spacious bathroom in a Connecticut home, my clients hoped to incorporate a sauna as part of a larger remodel. Although it was a long-standing wish list item for them, it would have immediately maxed out their budget. Instead of compromising on other design elements or sacrificing the quality or size of the sauna they'd been wanting, they made the decision to frame the sauna area and install the necessary wiring, but to outfit the space as a walk-in closet for the time being. When they're ready, they plan to fully realize their sauna dream. Don't be afraid to compromise on the timeline to reach your ultimate design vision.

How to DIY

The key to a successful DIY project is being realistic about what you are able to take on. Some people consider tiling a wall to be a DIY while others (myself included) max out on painting. Depending on your skill and confidence levels, DIY projects can be great ways to save money and learn new skills. But make sure you thoroughly research what the project entails (in terms of skill, materials, and time) to make sure that it really is something you can accomplish yourself. Talking to other people who have done similar projects on Reddit or Facebook can be helpful; my favorite way to learn how to do something is to watch YouTube videos. Always invest in the proper tools and equipment for the job; saving money on labor may be a great tactic for keeping costs low but if you aren't using the proper materials and end up needing to bring a professional in to fix your shoddy work, it can end up costing more than the project originally would have. Always wear the appropriate protective gear and follow safety rules!

Use Costly Materials Sparingly

Once you've chosen a wallpaper pattern, don't be afraid to commit to it, and consider different ways you can work it into your space. In a recent prewar Brooklyn townhouse, my clients wanted to add wallpaper into their nursery, but it was going to be a major splurge moment because of the high ceilings. We decided to install wainscoting in the room and wallpaper above it instead of going floor to ceiling. It was an elevated solution to our budgetary constraints that added another elegant layer into our design. On the other hand, I am not a fan of the accent wall (wallpapering a single wall and painting the others), which I think feels tentative and dated.

Where to Save vs. Where to Splurge

I believe a high-low method is the best way to approach interior design. Strategic splurge moments make an entire space look elevated and save you from feeling like you need to spend a fortune on every piece. While the way you attribute your budget will be personal for you, your space, and the way you use your home, there are some rules of thumb I abide by.

Investing in a sofa (see Rule #28) and mattress (see Rule #29) are worthwhile because it's critical that you can relax and sleep comfortably at home. Furniture pieces with functioning parts like drawers are worth splurging on because cheaper materials will break down quickly, and you'll end up replacing the piece and spending the money twice. But aside from these items, if you have to choose between investing in the work you do to alter your actual space versus spending money on furniture, it's more impactful to put the money toward the alterations to your space. Updating a room has the ability to elevate the ambiance surrounding drab furniture, while placing costly furniture in a drab room will just highlight how unfinished the space itself feels.

In a bathroom renovation, splurge on high-end fixtures and faucets, as these will make the bathroom feel upgraded, but save on an inexpensive, well-installed tile. In a kitchen, spring for the best appliances your budget allows for; if you do a panel front dishwasher or refrigerator, you don't need to worry about matching brands and can often find some savings that way.

Smart Shopping

Big-box furniture stores almost always have sales around holidays, so if you know you are going to be purchasing it's best to time your buys. Facebook Marketplace is an incredible resource for second-hand items; you can often find vintage designer pieces and even current, gently used pieces at a fraction of the cost. Shipping costs for furniture can be outrageous, so if a store gives you the option to set up your own freight (either picking up the piece yourself, through TaskRabbit, or using a third-party shipper like uShip) you can often save hundreds, if not thousands. When shopping in a retail store ask to purchase floor models; these gently-used pieces are usually in next-to-perfect condition and offer great price savings. As with clothing retailers, many designer furniture stores have sample sales. If you're eyeing something from a high-end store, ask to be added to their mailing list to receive notifications about these sales.

Borrow from Peter to Pay Paul

While it's imperative that you are comfortable with your total budget amount (including the 15 percent buffer), it is equally important not to restrict yourself by rigidly adhering to the prices you've set for each individual item. If the grand project total remains the same, you can reasonably spend more on one specific piece, so long as you spend less than you expected to elsewhere.

This is a trick I learned and adapted from my short-lived fashion career: pairing luxe accessories with more affordable clothing makes your entire look appear higher-end. In interiors, you can strategically elevate the look of a room by redistributing your budget to spend less on the larger items and splurge on the finer details that tie a space together. Say using your schedule you have established a $3,000 budget for setting up your bed: $2,000 bed frame, $600 mattress, $400 bedding. If instead you choose a simple, affordable bed frame ($800) and invest in a sumptuous mattress ($1,100) and delicious high-end linens ($1,100) the result is a lot more luxurious and elevated than it would be if you had used the bulk of the budget on a designer bed frame and sparsely outfitted it with a thin mattress, cheap sheets, and a limp throw pillow.

If your total budget for art is $350 ($300 art, $50 frame), you might consider purchasing a piece of affordable art from a flea market or Etsy ($30) and then framing it exquisitely ($320), which can make the whole composition feel more elevated. Or use an inexpensive lamp ($50) and splurge on the lampshade ($300) for a bespoke touch.

Using Mirrors to Your Advantage

This doesn't count as a design book until I start singing about the benefits of incorporating mirrors into your home. This design mainstay is as popular as it is for two reasons: Mirrors open walls so instead of your eye reading a flat surface, they read everything that is reflected into them. Also, mirrors bounce light around, and the brighter the space, the larger it appears. Place a lamp in front of a mirror or hang your mirror opposite a window; this makes it so that you are "adding" another lamp or window into your room and again—more lamps/windows mean more brightness and more brightness means bigger room.

Utilizing Color

If you've ever donned head-to-toe black in hopes of appearing slimmer, you understand the majestic shrinking powers of dark color. Use it when you want to make a space feel cozy. Or take the opposite approach and use bright colors to make a space appear larger.

 If you paint walls, trim, and ceiling the same color (a technique known as color drenching), it's harder for your eye to gauge where the wall stops and the ceiling starts; these blurred lines make a space feel a little larger.

Double-Duty Pieces

Sometimes the best approach to a smaller space means having fewer pieces of furniture. Less furniture means that each piece you include will need to serve multiple functions. A storage ottoman, for example, combines a surface, an extra place to perch, and storage all into the same piece.

Strategic Furniture

Clear furniture like glass or lucite feels weightless in a space and almost disappears, allowing your eye to see farther into the room and giving the illusion of a larger space. Similarly, furniture on legs (rather than sitting low on the ground) enables a clearer, longer line of sight.

Play with Scale

Often the temptation when working on a smaller space is to use smaller furniture; it may be counterintuitive but by using an oversize piece of furniture in a smaller room, you create a focal point in the space that makes it feel grander. For example, using an impressive cabinet in a small foyer makes the space feel more important and elevated.

Maximize Storage to Minimize Clutter

Nothing makes a room feel claustrophobic as quickly as clutter does. Edit your items, make sure that you have a designated spot for everything, and include ample hidden storage.

Get It Off the Floor

Using a light source that takes up zero floor space (such as a sconce, table lamp, or overhead lighting) saves room in your floor plan. Sneak in shelves everywhere you can to keep objects off the floor. Get creative with where you are placing shelves; consider places like above a doorframe, over a radiator, over a bed, or above a sofa.

Settle Into Symmetry

Symmetry is visually calming to the eye. It lets your brain process information more quickly. The faster your eye can move through a space, the larger it appears.

Childproof Aesthetically

Family moments are much easier to enjoy when you aren't stressing about your kids hurting themselves or ruining your furniture. Childproofing is a combination of selecting practical furniture and materials, including aesthetically pleasing safety features, and teaching your kids how to respect belongings. A couple of tips:

"Fast furniture" (think IKEA and similar vendors) is more likely to tip over than well-made, heavier, (often) older pieces. In all cases, tall pieces should be secured to walls properly. Similarly, make sure that side tables are heavy enough that a child can't knock them over. Move items off the coffee table until you can teach your baby not to grab.

Buying vintage furniture that already has a level of distress or "patina" will camouflage new marks that your kids make. Patterned fabrics and rugs hide more stains than flat solids. Make sure surfaces that are reachable by babies aren't prone to visible fingerprints.

Magnetic cabinet locks are invisible and extremely easy to install, and self-closing outlet covers are cleaner looking than the little plastic inserts.

If you have little kids, install child-lock mechanisms on window shades to make sure there are no dangling cords or pulls.

Family-Friendly Fabrics

I recommend Fiber-Seal to almost all of my clients, families or not. It is a Greenguard-certified (see Rule #87) concentration that is professionally sprayed onto almost any kind of upholstery to make stains pool on the surface for easy cleaning. Materials like Sunbrella, Perennials, and Crypton are specifically formulated to withstand wear and tear. Wool is a very strong natural material. Leather is resistant to stains because you can wipe it, but it will show scratches. Slipcovers are amazing because you can use whatever fabric you want, and if a bad spill happens, you just take it to the dry cleaner, or, better yet, throw it in the wash.

Independent Play and Cleanup

I firmly believe that at the end of the day, when kids are asleep, toys should be put away so that your space feels like a place for adults. Children can't take part in the cleanup process if they can't access the designated storage areas for their belongings, so organize your home in a way that promotes independence. Kid-height shelves help them easily see their toys and take responsibility for tidying up. Natural-material bins and baskets maintain toy organization without compromising aesthetics, and lidded hampers serve as a convenient place for stashing stuffed animals. One key to concealing toys in plain sight is to keep items out of an average adult's line of vision; for example, a low open shelf in a coffee table can be an ideal spot for storing board games or puzzles. Montessori-style bookshelves, facing out to show book covers, enable a child to reach for a book independently. Remove markers and crayons from their boxes and put them in decorative bins or baskets to keep art supplies in order and more aesthetically pleasing.

Designing a Kid's Bedroom

Kids' bedrooms are far and away my favorite rooms to design. There is liberty in designing these rooms that you just don't get anywhere else. The key to designing a successful kid's room is striking the delicate balance of creating an imaginative, vibrant space that will also grow and evolve alongside the child.

I love to use wallpaper in a kid's space, but fun paint colors also work beautifully; consider painting the trim in a contrasting color for even more whimsy. That said, kids naturally accumulate many colorful belongings like toys and books, so leaning toward muted tones in furniture and wall coverings won't necessarily result in a sterile or boring room. If you have your heart set on a pattern that may soon be declared "babyish," consider using it in their bathroom or playroom as kids tend to tolerate things for longer outside of their bedrooms. I love to incorporate antique pieces in children's rooms because they add warmth and character. Bins and baskets in natural materials keep a kid's room from feeling like a toy store or a preschool.

Ultimately, a child's bedroom should reflect their personality, so let them have a say into what goes into their space. The trick is to gently usher them toward the more sophisticated version of whatever it is they're currently coveting, so that the design has longevity and they find joy in the room for years to come.

Pet Practices

Your pets don't have to cramp your style. You just have to keep them in mind as you make choices throughout the house and set up a dedicated space within your home for your pet's toys and blankets. To keep things organized, use lidded baskets, like how you might for children's toys. Choose toys and a bed for your pet that blend seamlessly with your furniture. Cats tend to claw at textural fabrics and can rip leather with their claws so flatter weaves are better for them, while leathers are good for dogs because stains can be wiped off. And remember that some popular house plants are toxic to pets so when you get a new plant, make sure you are aware of potential hazards. A little design trick I like is to create a slipcover for a dog bed using one of the fabrics featured elsewhere in the room. This adds a cheeky touch and makes the entire space feel cohesive and intentional. It also turns a nondescript dog bed into a conversation piece.

A few years ago I helped a friend design her home in Greenwich Village. Our goal for the apartment was to turn it into a chic Parisian-inspired super-feminine space. One of the bolder design decisions we made was to stain her parquet floors a dark glossy black resembling ebony piano keys. PSA: Do not stain your floors black and then adopt a 70-pound white dog. Six months into pet parental bliss, my friend was finding new scratches on her floor every day. We ended up replacing her flooring with engineered white oak herringbone, which was scratch-resistant and camouflaged the hair.

Reclaimed and Recycled Furniture

Not only is it more sustainable to purchase reclaimed furniture, but the quality of construction is almost always better, too. Antique pieces have had a long life, which is a good indication of their strength and durability. (See Rule #25 for more on antiques and vintage furniture.)

The trick to scoring a good recycled find is to look past imperfections and focus on the potential. My favorite chair in my own home is one I found at Merchant House, a vintage dealer in New Orleans. The wood chair was only $50 because it was missing an arm. It was affordable and easy for me to find someone on TaskRabbit who was able to make and attach a new arm. The chair looks great, and the slight arm mismatch only adds to the charm.

When it comes to vintage upholstered pieces, you'll almost always want to reupholster the item with your choice of fabric. Therefore, look past the condition and pattern of the fabric and focus instead on the overall silhouette of the piece. Remember, it's easy for an upholsterer to remove or change channeling or tufting.

If you're not yet confident in your ability to pick out large vintage pieces from the treasure heap, a great place to start is with accessories. This helps you determine which stores and styles resonate with you and can guide your search for larger items. Chairish features curated edits from leading designers, so if you feel overwhelmed by all the options on their site, visit your favorite designers' page to see what Chairish's editors are choosing.

When you find something in an antiques shop, visualize where you will use it in your home. If you have a specific spot in mind, it's a safer purchase than impulse buying something you love without a dedicated place for it.

Energy-Efficient Home Design

Creating an energy-efficient home is not only beneficial for the environment, it's also cost effective. While incorporating energy-efficient systems can be initially expensive, many improvements eventually pay for themselves through savings on your energy bills. If you're interested in implementing some sustainable design solutions but aren't sure where to start, check for available rebates and incentives in your area. There are often promotions for installing electric car chargers, solar panels, and geothermal heating. You can prioritize how to upgrade your home systems based on when these programs become available in your area. Replace any standard single-pane glass windows in your home with thicker glass to insulate your space and regulate temperatures; to conserve water, replace your existing appliances with low-flow toilets, faucets, and showerheads.

When you're building a new home, there are various options to achieve energy efficiency, ranging from standard energy-efficient designs to "net zero," or even "net positive," homes. These designs usually encompass a well-sealed building envelope, self-sustaining heating and cooling systems, energy-generation solutions, and even rainwater collection and reuse.

Ethical and Eco-Friendly Furniture Certifications

When shopping for new furniture, look for certifications to ensure that products meet certain sustainability and ethical standards. Certifications will vary by area but the main ones to look for are:

- **C2C (Cradle to Cradle):** This certification assesses the environmental footprint of a product throughout its entire life cycle. Products with this certification were intentionally designed for maximum sustainability.

- **FSC (Forest Stewardship Council):** This certification means that the wood used to make the product was sourced or farmed responsibly.

- **GOTS (Global Organic Textile Standard):** Used on upholstered pieces, GOTS is basically to fabric what FSC is to wood.

- **Greenguard:** This certification measures a product's chemical emissions and off-gassing.

- **Fair Trade:** Signifies that goods were made in an ethical, safe, work environment. This certification is not specific to furniture or the home industry.

Choosing Sustainable Building Materials

Sustainable building choices lower the carbon footprint of your home and make updating your space more environmentally responsible.

- Incorporating **reclaimed wood, metal, bricks, and stones** in your design adds a rich, storied quality that a new material simply cannot deliver.

- **FSC-certified wood** reduces deforestation, so when buying new hardwood flooring make sure it has that certification.

- **Bamboo** is quick to grow, so it is a highly sustainable choice for flooring and cabinetry.

- VOCs (volatile organic compounds) are gases that contribute to bad indoor air quality. Choose **low- or no-VOC paints, stains, and cleaning supplies**, which are not only environmentally conscious, but better for the health of your family.

Local Sourcing and Artisanal Makers

There are many advantages—environmental and otherwise—to buying your furniture from local, smaller makers or boutiques. In addition to reducing emissions associated with long-distance or overseas shipping, short shipping distances often require less packaging materials, and therefore less waste. Shopping locally also supports your community's economy and offers a chance to speak directly to furniture makers; this helps ensure you're getting exactly what you need, reducing the chance you will need to replace an incorrect or a damaged-in-transit item.

Containing Closet Clutter

The first step in having an organized closet is making the most of the space itself and personalizing it for your needs. Of course, you can install a custom closet system with a professional who will come to your home, measure your space, customize the design, and oversee its installation. But there are also some easy DIY ways to optimize your closet:

- Add a lower hanging rod to create more hanging storage.

- Purchase hanging shelves for folded clothes.

- Acrylic shelf dividers go a long way in keeping purses and smaller accessories organized so you can see everything.

- Hanging jewelry in clear containers makes it easy to access and assess what you own.

- Label bins in the closet to remember what goes where. When the seasons change, you should reorganize your closet so that you aren't cluttering your space with items that you can't wear. This could mean moving summer items onto higher, harder to reach shelves in the winter or removing the off-season items from your closet altogether and storing them in under-bed bins, or in a closet in another room.

- Matching hangers make everything feel more pulled together. Space-saving hangers are especially useful so your clothes are not crammed together.

- Utilize as much vertical space as you can and add a shelf at the very top of your closet for thinner, folded clothes or lesser-used items like scarves or bathing suits organized in shallow bins or trays.

Also, remember the interior of your closet can be a fun design moment just like anywhere else. Paint it with a fun pop of color, install extravagant wallpaper, or add a special light fixture to help your closet feel like a room of its own instead of just a utilitarian storage area.

Two of my favorite rules for keeping a closet organized are the like-with-like rule and the one-in-one-out rule. The like-with-like rule means similar items should be grouped together in your closet. The one-in-one-out rule means that when you get something new, you need to make room for it by donating or selling something you already own.

Picture-Perfect Pantry

When organizing your pantry, the first step is to remove everything and sift through it. Discard any expired or stale food. Next, wipe down the pantry to make sure you are setting a clean foundation for the new organization system you are about to implement. Group items by type so that they are easy to find. Some examples might include: canned goods, specialty soups and sauces, savory snacks, sweet snacks. Purchase acrylic bins (the transparency makes it easier to find what you're looking for) and label them. Group similar bins together: put savory snacks near sweet snacks; pastas near grains, etc. Add additional shelves if the ones you have aren't adequate. Make it a habit to regularly sift through and discard expired items.

Kitchen spices should be alphabetized; it's satisfying and makes finding spices so much easier. Keep a separate bin labeled "extra spices" in the pantry for duplicates.

Your At-Home Spa

One of the most common requests I hear from clients embarking on a renovation is that they want their bathroom to feel "spa-like." One of the easiest adjustments you can make to your bathroom to make it more relaxing is to keep it organized. Many toiletries expire just like groceries so go through your cabinets and get rid of anything that is either no longer usable or that you are likely never going to want to use again. Once you have gotten rid of unwanted items, make piles based on use; for example, make a "hair product" section, a "face product" section, etc. Within those piles, separate items you use everyday and put those in an easy-to-access place; if you have a medicine cabinet, this could mean eye level in the medicine cabinet. If you don't have a medicine cabinet, you may put these items in a bin labeled "everyday." Keep the other items in labeled acrylic bins. While it's best not to have too much visible "stuff" in your bathroom, you will want some items to remain on your countertop like your toothbrush and hand soap. Keep these items in coordinating containers on a tray so they feel unified and organized. If you are sharing a bathroom with a few people, it may make sense for everyone to have their own caddy they can pull out from underneath the sink.

Entryway Essentials

An entryway is an important room in your home because it's the chance to make a first impression. Organize the interior of your entryway closet so that every member of your household has a designated place to hang their coat and put their shoes away. If you don't have a coat closet, you will probably want to add hooks into your entryway. There are a lot of sculptural, beautiful hooks available and these can be another opportunity to add personality to your space. They can also be a fun moment to incorporate something vintage. Try not to overcrowd coat hooks because they will look cluttered; instead let everyone in your family have one dedicated hook and hang other jackets elsewhere, if you can.

A beautiful console table or vintage dresser provides storage space for trinkets, pet leashes, and cold weather accessories. Make sure that there's a sense of purpose to vessels on your surface space so you have a designated place to store mail and keys. Layer in fresh flowers and striking art to set the tone for the rest of your home.

Finesse Your Front Door

Your front door hardware is the first tactile impression you'll have of your space so invest in hardware that feels heavyweight and that makes you happy. Splash a rich paint color on your front door to express your personal sense of style and set the tone for your house; it will make people want to see more of what's inside.

The Art of Setting the Dinner Table

A tablescape is an important component in making your home entertaining-ready because it communicates to guests that you care about them and that you put in effort to make their dinner special.

At a minimum, every tablescape should include plates, bowls, and drinking glasses for each guest, as well as utensils and a napkin. A more elaborate tablescape might also include a tablecloth or runner, centerpieces, flowers, chargers or placemats, place cards, menus, napkin rings, and candles. No matter how simple or over-the-top you decide to make your tablescape, you should set it up a few days before the gathering so on the day of, you can focus on getting other elements of your party ready. Dressing up your table in advance also gives you the chance to tweak the design as you sit with it.

The first step in creating a tablescape is to establish the color palette. Your color palette doesn't need to match the dining room, but it should complement the colors and feel of your space. You can use a monochromatic color scheme to keep things simple and streamlined or use a more dynamic color scheme (think mixing and matching colors) to build a layered look. If you don't know where to start with a color palette, look to nature and build something seasonal, as this will always feel appropriate. If you have a garden, pulling greenery from outside is a cost-free way of livening up your table. Florals and brightly colored fruit make a table come to life; a tablescape should be a place to have fun, so don't be afraid to get creative and add a little va-va-voom.

Building a collection of tableware over time ensures your table feels storied and personal and enables you to mix and match pieces to set the right mood for your party. Don't forget to incorporate different

textures and patterns into your tablescape. Placemats or chargers add a sculptural element underneath each place setting and help define each person's space.

Remember scale when building your tablescape; while oversize floral arrangements and extra-tall candlesticks are beautiful in theory, they get in the way of making conversation during intimate dinner parties at home. A few small simple, low floral arrangements create an inexpensive, pulled-together look that is easy to have conversation over and serve food around. I like to use a mixture of taper candles, structured pillar candles, and some tea lights to create a festive glow.

Snuggle Up

It's important to visually activate the bed with interesting bedding. If your entire room is "designed" but your bed has plain white sheets, it's going to feel like a void in the middle of the room. Conversely, if you're trying to create a crisp, tailored aesthetic, clean white sheets can be the perfect bedding for underscoring the edited mood you're trying to create.

In my opinion, it's always best to opt for light-colored sheets, even if the rest of the textile story is darker: they just feel cleaner and fresher to me. Sheets can be made of many different materials; but the main ones are percale, linen, and sateen. You may want to have a couple different materials on hand for changing seasonal temperatures, as some are a lot heavier than others.

- **Percale** sheets are classic and cool-feeling, so people who tend to get hot when they sleep generally find them to be most comfortable. These are what you think of when you imagine crisp hotel sheets.

- **Linen** is an ancient Egyptian cloth that comes from the flax plant. Its natural quick moisture-wicking properties makes it great in humid, warm environments; and also make it a preferred material for hot sleepers. Linen has an easy-breezy look (or as some would say, wrinkles easily), so if you're looking for something polished, this isn't the fabric for you. Linen is usually scratchier-feeling than percale or sateen sheets, but softens over time as you use and wash your sheets.

- **Sateen** sheets are warmer and heavier than percale or linen. They have a silk-like sheen and feel very smooth. If you are someone who has a set of winter sheets and a set of summer sheets, sateen's thermal properties make them a smart winter option.

But sheets aren't the only things that go into making a bed:

- **Duvets** come in a multitude of weights, so you may want to have a winter option and a summer option here, or ditch the duvet altogether in favor of a coverlet or quilt if you live in a warm climate. A duvet is a great place to add texture and interest to your bedding scheme.

- **Throw blankets** are a perfect opportunity to add a special pattern, color, or material into your bedroom. Since these are more decorative and less functional, you can use something more fragile like an embroidered or antique textile, if you like.

As for pillows, I prefer fewer, smaller decorative pillows in the bedroom. It's just not practical to be moving excessive shams out of the way every time you need to lie down.

Artful Picture Hanging

A house doesn't feel like a home until there is art on the walls. It's one of my design pet peeves when people won't put art on a wall because they've wallpapered it. Hanging art on wallpaper makes your space feel finished. If you really don't want to put a hole into the wall, install a picture rail (see Rule #44).

In most cases, art should be hung at eye level, so I usually recommend hanging the middle of a picture around 65 inches from the ground. If you're hanging art above a piece of furniture, make sure the art isn't more than a few inches from the furniture's top surface; it will feel "off" if your art is

floating too far away. I used to work with someone who always said small art on a big wall looks like a pimple. The visual has stuck in my mind and informed my opinion that it's almost always better to scale up.

A gallery wall is an artful arrangement of many different pieces of art displayed on a single wall. These can be organized in a grid pattern with matching frames for a more formal look, or asymmetrically in mismatched frames to add a bit of whimsy. Gallery walls are effective in pulling your eye through a space, so they are particularly suitable for hallways and staircases. I always recommend hiring a professional to hang art, however if you are trying to DIY a gallery wall, arrange your pieces on the floor first to plan out spacing and composition. Start by positioning the larger frames and then plug in the holes with smaller pieces. It can be fun and impactful to maximize vertical wall space on a gallery wall, so feel free to break the rules and place artwork near the floor or close to the ceiling. This will almost have the effect of creating your own wallpaper.

Scents and Aromatherapy

Design is not just about visual elements. Fragrance also makes a strong impression when you walk into a space. Line your stored linens with dryer sheets, bars of soap, aromatherapy bars, or even tea bags to infuse them with a subtle aroma and to fight musty odors. Lavender can be a particularly good choice for this, as it is known to deter moths. When you open the sheets to make the bed there will be a burst of freshness. You can do this with your off-season clothing as well. I love scented candles and aromatherapy diffusers, particularly ones that are seasonally appropriate and contained in beautiful vessels.

Throw Pillow Know-How

Early in my career, clients hired me to do smaller jobs that usually boiled down to "tying a room together." More often than not this really meant they wanted me to help them pick out pillows. Accent pillows on a sofa, daybed, lounge chair, or bed make a room feel layered and warm. They can totally change the vibe of a space and are easy to swap out when you want to give your room a quick pick-me-up. You don't need to overdo it with pillows; a few simple, striking layers can make a big difference and feel tailored and edited. The trick is to create an environment that feels both livable and textural.

Pairing matching sets of pillows on either side of the sofa is traditional and can be beautiful, but it's more dynamic to build a story around textiles you love instead of worrying too much about perfect pairs. If you want a DIY project, you can make throw pillow covers out of

textiles or a piece of antique fabric. If you are trying to create a calmer mood, choose colors that are the same tone as your sofa. If you want something more energizing, use a contrasting color instead.

Decide on the number of pillows you want to use; for a standard sofa, I like three or five, as the asymmetric nature feels playful and laid back. The more pillows you have, the more traditional your space will feel. For a more modern mood, you may only want two pillows, perhaps made from the same fabric as your sofa for an even more streamlined look. The pillows should complement the size of your sofa; the largest I like to use is 22 × 22 inches for standard pillows or 20 × 12 inches for lumbar pillows. Aim to include variety in size: layer in 20 × 20-inch pillows or 18 × 18-inch pillows to bounce the eye around and make your pillows feel collected.

Stack Your Shelves

Every home needs books. Like art, books make a space feel lived in. They tell a story about the people who live in the home and make a space feel cozy. Books can be organized on bookcases or stacked on surfaces to add layers to a space. Some people like to organize their books in rainbow order while others are absolutely horrified by that idea. To me, having books is significantly more important than wringing your hands over the way the books are arranged. In homes with multiple living spaces, I love to designate one room as a reading room or library; there's nothing cozier than an entire room dedicated to curling up and reading.

Acknowledgments

When I'm not engaged in design work, one of my favorite pastimes has always been reading. Nothing feels more tranquil to me than spending an afternoon immersed in a book, and writing one has long been an aspiration of mine. The idea of walking into a bookstore and seeing my own book on the shelves alongside those of authors I admire was something I never even dared to vocalize. So when my now editor, Amanda Englander, emailed me in July 2022 with the subject line "book project?" I almost dismissed it as spam, but on a whim forwarded it to my trusted publicist, Christina Cattarini, with a two-word email: "fake, right?" So, firstly, I want to express my gratitude to Christina for encouraging me to respond to Amanda's email ("Seems legit! Worth a call for sure!"), and to Amanda and the rest of the Union Square & Co. team—Caitlin Leffel, Ivy McFadden, Renée Bollier—for trusting me with bringing *House Rules* to fruition. As someone without professional writing experience, I've found your guidance throughout this process invaluable.

I also wish to extend my heartfelt thanks to all of my wonderful clients, who afford me the opportunity to pursue my passion every day. I understand that renovating your dream homes marks a significant milestone in your lives, and the trust you place in me to guide you through it means the world to me.

To my mom: Thank you for instilling in me a love for bold style from a young age, for allowing me to experiment with design in my room and our home as a child, but above all, for always encouraging me to pursue my dreams and for raising me to believe that I am capable of anything.

And, of course, to my husband, Ben, and our children, Rosie and Caleb: Words cannot express my appreciation.